God's Story 3

told by the People of God

———— SECOND EDITION ————

God's Story 3 | Second Edition
A Catholic Project Title

Published by Rejoice Publications 2017
an imprint of
Matthew James Publishing Ltd,
Unit 46, Goyt Mill
Upper Hibbert Lane
Marple, SK6 7HX

ISBN13: 978-1-910265-34-5

First Edition published 2002
Reprinted 2004, 2007, 2010
Revised edition published 2014
2nd Edition published 2017

© Catholic Education Service

Nihil obstat George Stokes, Censor
Imprimatur Rt Rev Thomas McMahon, Bishop of Brentwood
Brentwood 14 April 2002

The Nihil obstat and imprimatur are a declaration that a book or pamphlet is considered to be free from doctrinal or moral error. It is not implied that those who have granted the Nihil obstat or Imprimatur agree with the contents, opinions or statements expressed.

All rights reserved. No part of this publication may be reproduced or stored or transmitted by any means or in any form, electronic or mechanical, including photocopying, recording or any information storage and retrieval system without written permission which should be sought from the publisher.

Photo credits
© iStock: 6, 10, 13, 15, 16, 21, 22, 33, 41, 45, 46, 48, 55, 56, 57, 61, 62, 63, 66, 67, 77, 83, 85, 87, 91, 135, 139, 141, 143, 144, 146, 149
© Shutterstock: 13, 16, 32, 35, 43, 44, 108, 148
© David Lund: 39, 42, 45, 47, 52, 60, 90, 95, 106, 117
© Fotolia: 44, 110, 125

For more detailed information regarding image licences, please contact us through www.matthewjamespublishing.com

Illustrations by Kati Teague
Design and page layout based on original by Peter Robb

Contents

Welcome 5
The Bible 6

THE OLD TESTAMENT

The Book of Genesis — 7
  In the Beginning — 8
  Made to be like God — 10
  The Seventh Day — 10
  Abraham — 12
  Father of a great people — 12
  The Promised Son: Isaac — 12
  The deaths of Sarah and Abraham — 13
  Esau and Jacob — 14
  The Children of Israel — 14
  Joseph — 15

The Book of Exodus — 18
  Trouble in Egypt — 19
  God chooses Moses — 20
  The Escape to Freedom — 21
  Journey to the Promised Land — 24
  God's Commandments — 26

The Books of Deuteronomy & Leviticus — 28
  Tell your children — 29
  A song of the journey — 29
  Care for others — 30
  And God said — 30

The Books of Samuel and the Kings — 32
  The birth of Samuel — 33
  The call of Samuel — 34
  God's prophet — 34
  The First King — 34
  David is chosen — 35
  David and Solomon — 36

  Ruth — 37
  The Temple — 38

The Book of Psalms — 40
  Pilgrimage Psalms — 42
  Prayers for help — 44
  Trust in God's love — 46
  Creation Psalms — 48
  Praise and Thanksgiving — 52

The Wisdom Books — 53
  Proverbs — 54
  Song of Songs — 54
  Ecclesiasticus — 55
  Ecclesiastes — 55

The Books of the Prophets — 58
  The Promised One — 59
  Bringer of peace — 59
  Strong and true — 60
  Let the whole world be glad! — 61
  Here is yo ur God — 62
  God's People — 63
  Here I am — 64
  Good News for the poor — 65
  God is coming — 65
  God Says ... — 66
  I will forgive you — 66
  Change! — 66
  My love for you is great — 67
  Make sure justice is for all — 67
  God sings for joy! — 67

The New Testament

The Gospels — 68
    The Coming of Jesus — 69
    A Family Tree — 69
    The Announcement of John's birth — 70
    The Annunciation to Mary — 71
    The Visitation — 72
    The Birth of John — 73
    The Birth of Jesus — 74
    The Shepherds — 75
    Wise Men — 76
    Joseph's dream — 77
    The Presentation — 78
    My Father's House — 79
    You are my Son — 80
    In the beginning — 81

The Gospel according to Matthew — 82
    A New Way of Living — 82
    Go Further — 84
    Teachings About ... — 85
    Remember! — 87
    A Parable — 88

The Gospel according to Mark — 89
    Good News of God — 89
    I have chosen you — 90
    An invitation — 91
    What does God want? — 92
    If you want to be my friend — 92
    I have come to give my life — 93

The Gospel according to Luke — 94
    When the time had come — 94
    Jesus begins his mission — 95
    Jesus calls Levi — 96
    Jesus feeds the people — 96
    Jesus gives sight to a blind man — 98
    Jesus forgives a sinner — 98
    The Women — 99
    Who is my neighbour? — 100
    Parable of the prodigal son — 102
    Lord, teach us to pray — 104
    The Good Shepherd — 104
    The Pharisee and the tax collector — 104

The Gospel according to John — 105
    Finding Jesus — 105
    Jesus the Bread of Life — 106
    Who is a sinner? — 107
    Words of Life — 108
    Remain in my love — 109
    The Promise of the Spirit — 109
    Jesus' prayer for his friends — 109
    The True Vine — 110

The Greatest Week — 112
    From death to life — 112
    The time is near — 113
    Palm Sunday — 113
    Holy Thursday — 114
    Washing of the feet — 115
    Gethsemane — 116
    Good Friday — 118
    Jesus is sent to Herod — 119
    On the way to Calvary — 120
    The Thieves — 121
    The Death of Jesus — 122
    Jesus and his mother — 123
    The Burial of Jesus — 124

The Empty Tomb — 125

New Life: A New Beginning — 128
    On the road to Emmaus — 128
    Jesus appears to his friends — 130
    Go out all over the world — 130

The Acts of the Apostles — 131
    The Ascension — 132
    Pentecost — 132
    The New People of God — 134
    We cannot keep silent — 136
    Sharing the mission — 137
    People and Places — 138

Spreading the Good News — 140
    Letters from Paul — 143
    Letters from Peter — 149
    Letters from John — 149

The Book of Revelation — 150
    Notes for Adults — 153

Welcome

Dear Children,

In this book, you will discover God's Story. Long before it was written down it was told by fathers and mothers and grandparents and aunts and uncles.

People wanted to tell their children about the love and goodness of God. They wanted them to discover that God was with them and cared for them.

Those who had met Jesus wanted everyone to know him and how important he is in the story of God's love.

These stories are part of the story of the whole human family. The Holy Spirit helps the Church family to treasure them. The words of the people who believed in God over thousands of years are remembered and celebrated every day. Everywhere, priests and people read, pray and study the message of God's love for the whole world.

You are part of the story of the human family. I hope you will enjoy learning about the story of God's love and of the faithful men and women who believed in God. I hope you will discover many things to encourage you and help you to grow in trust and love for God and the world and all its people.

✝ Edwin Regan
Bishop Emeritus
Former Chairman of the National Project

The Bible

The word 'Bible' means 'book' although, strictly speaking, it is not one book but a library of books.

The books of the Old Testament tell of the events which prepared for the coming of Jesus. The books of the New Testament tell of the birth, life, passion, death and resurrection of Jesus. They tell the story of Pentecost, the 'birthday' of the Church, and how the Church grew and spread.

The Old Testament was written in Hebrew and the New Testament in Greek. The Bible has been translated many times, and there are different versions.

The books of the Bible were written over many centuries. Some of the people who wrote them did not bother much about dates, so nobody knows exactly when they were written. We do know that it took a thousand years or more for all the books to be completed. The first books were written around the tenth century BC, and the last book was written at the end of the first century AD.

Many different writers took up the story. Each wrote in his own way, so you will find poetry, prayer, letters, history, documentaries, drama, legend and biography – most of the kinds of writing that you will find in any good library.

The Bible is the story of God's love and how God's People responded to that love. There are many different kinds of writing, but all authors want to tell one thing: the Truth about God. God's Holy Spirit guided and inspired them in their work as authors. 'Inspire' means 'to breathe into'. The Church family believes that by the power of the Holy Spirit the words of the Bible are alive and life-giving. So the Church family prays for the Holy Spirit to guide its understanding of God's Word.

A Hebrew scribe transcribing the Word of God with care and attention as scribes have done for thousands of years.

GENESIS

Different strands of stories are woven together in this one book.

They tell us about a world and a special way of life which God offered to chosen people.

They tell of the Holy God the people worship.

They speak of the mystery of God who is greater than anyone can know.

They remind people that each person is made in the image of God.

He wrote a poem to tell everyone about the goodness of God and the world.......

A long time ago there was a holy and wise priest who loved God very much. He loved the people too and wanted them to know how much God loved and cared for them. He thought about the world and everything in it, how good it was – the rivers and seas full of fish; the skies full of flying creatures; the land full of animals of every shape and size; the earth full of rocks and stones. All these things God had given to people. He wrote a poem to tell everyone about the goodness of God and the world.

Genesis

IN THE BEGINNING (based on Genesis 1:1-25)

In the beginning, God created the sky and the land.
Everything was dark.
So God said, "Let there be light."
And there was light.
God saw that it was good.
God called the light 'day' and the darkness 'night'.

>God said, "Let there be water."
>And so it was. God called the
>dry land 'earth' and the water 'sea' and
>God saw that it was good.

God said, "Let the earth be filled with plants and trees." And so it was.
Plants and trees grew on earth full of fruit and vegetables.
God saw that it was good.

>God said, "Let there be two great lights in the sky.
>A great light to shine in the day,
>and a smaller light to shine in the night."
>God made the stars too.
>God saw that it was good.

God said, "Let the seas be filled with living creatures
and the skies be filled with flying creatures."
And so it was.
Great sea creatures and every kind of
winged creature filled the seas and skies.
God saw that it was good.

>God said, "Let the earth be filled with
>every kind of living creatures; wild animals
>and tame, reptiles that crawl on the earth."
>And so it was. God filled the world with
>every kind of animal and reptile.
>God saw that it was good.

Genesis

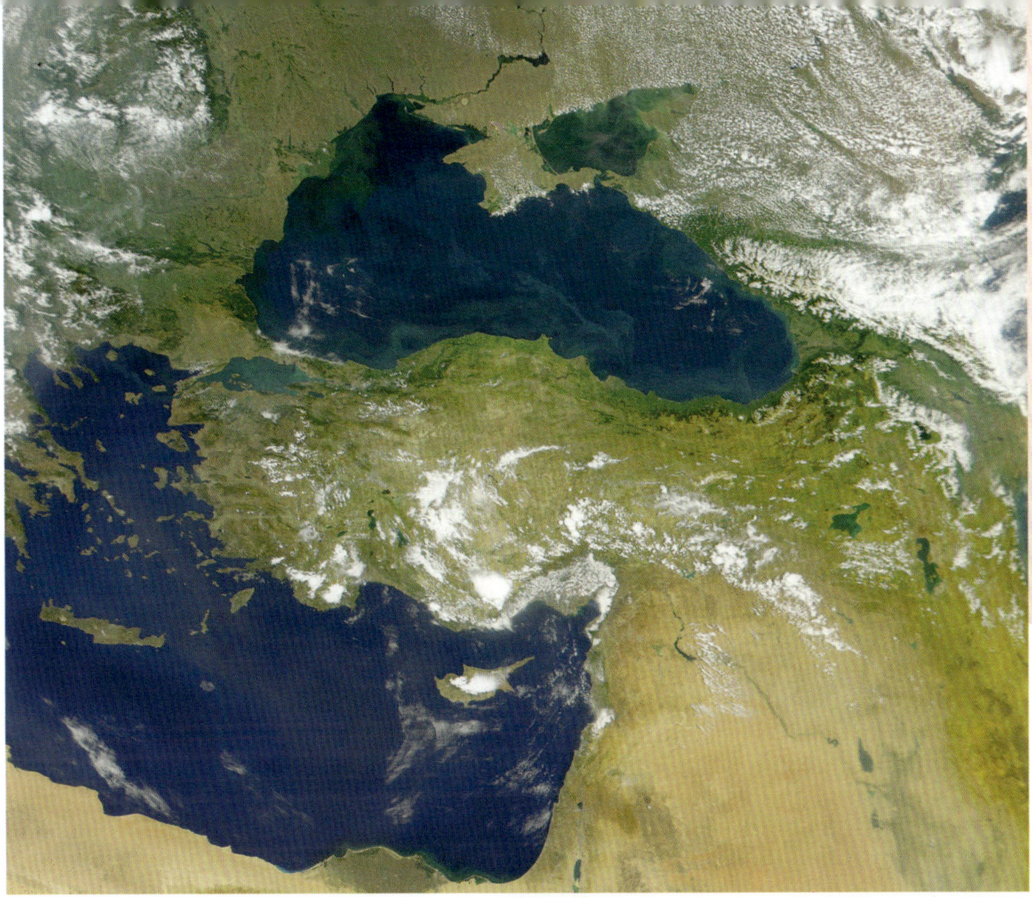

How did the world begin?

Scientists are always discovering more about our beginnings and the origins and history of our world.

Some scientists think the world began about five thousand million years ago; that life began about two thousand million years ago, and that human life began about three million years ago. You may like to find out what the latest ideas are about this.

Above: *The eastern Mediterranean and lands of the Bible seen from space.*

Right: *Today we can photograph the sun with a space telescope and know that an astronaut has left a footprint on the moon.*

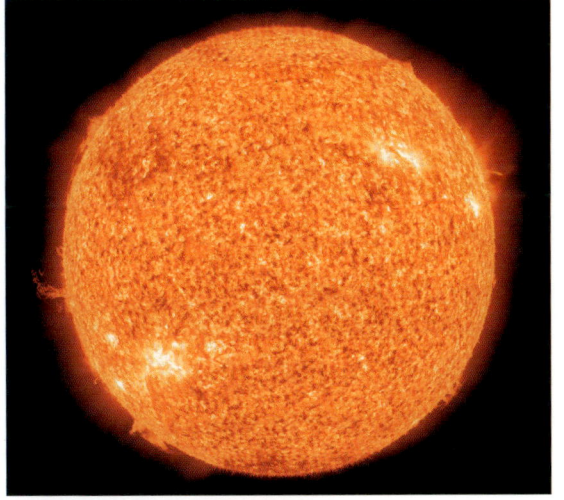

Genesis

MADE TO BE LIKE GOD

(based on Genesis 1:26-31)

Then God said: "Let us make people to be like ourselves. Men and women who can know and love me and know and love one another; and I will give them charge of the fish of the seas, the birds of the sky, and all the animals wild and tame and all the reptiles that crawl upon the earth."

So God created men and women who could love and care for the world and everything in it and could love and care for one another; men and women who could know God and love and serve God.

God blessed them and said to them:

"Fill the world with people; look after the world; look after one another; take care of the fish and the birds, the animals and the reptiles, the trees and the flowers and the plants."

And so it was.

God saw all creation, and indeed it was very good.

The Sabbath day

For the Jewish people, the seventh day (Saturday) is holy because it is the day of God's rest and is God's gift to them. For Christians, the first day of the week (Sunday) became the holy day because it was on that day that God his Father gave Jesus new life.

For Jews and Christians, marriage is holy because man and woman were created by God to love one another.

THE SEVENTH DAY

(based on Genesis 2:1-3)

After the work of creation, God rested on the seventh day. God blessed the seventh day and made it holy. And that is how the universe was created.

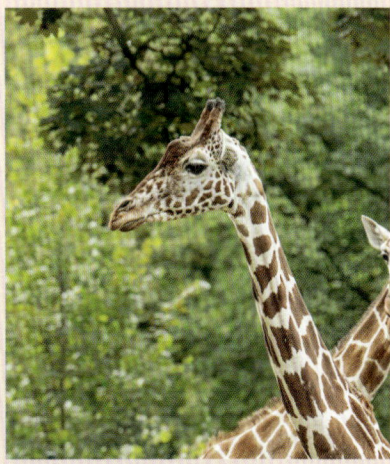

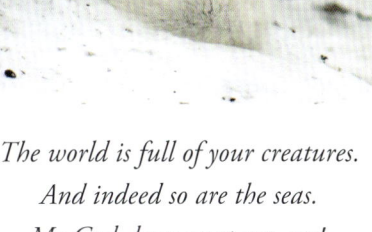

The world is full of your creatures.
And indeed so are the seas.
My God, how great you are!
(Ps 104)

Genesis 11

Genesis also tells the story of the beginnings of the Chosen People and the men and women who were the fathers and mothers of the nation. One of these was called Abram, which means 'great father'. God chose him to be the father of God's People.

ABRAHAM (based on Genesis 12:1-8, 18)

God spoke to Abram. "Leave your country, your relatives and your family home and go to a land I will show you. I will bless you, and make you a great and famous nation. All the people on earth will be blessed through you."

Abram was 75 years old when he left Haran. He took his wife, Sarai, his nephew Lot, his sheep and goats and all his possessions and set off for Canaan. When Abram arrived there, he went as far as Shechem the holy place called the Oak of Mamre. It was there that God told Abram that he was going to give all this land to him and his family. Abram built an altar there and worshipped God.

FATHER OF A GREAT PEOPLE (based on Genesis 15:2, 5-6, 18; 17:5, 15)

Some time later Abram was puzzling about God's promise because he had no children.

God said to him, "Don't worry. Look at the sky and count the stars if you can. You cannot possibly count them there are so many. Well, that is how many will be in your family."

Abram trusted God. It was his trust in God that made him a holy man.

That day God gave a solemn promise to Abram. "I will give your descendants all the land from the border of Egypt to the river Euphrates."

God said, "From now on your name will be Abraham because you will be the father of a great people. Your wife, Sarai, will be called Sarah, the mother of nations."

THE PROMISED SON: ISAAC (based on Genesis 21:1-7)

When their son was born, Sarah and Abraham remembered God's promise. They named the baby 'Isaac' which means 'he laughs', so his name became a reminder of God's blessing and their baby brought them great joy. On the day that Isaac was weaned, Abraham and Sarah gave a great feast to celebrate having a son.

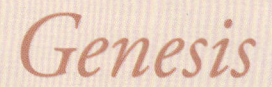

Genesis

Right: A Bedouin tent.
Below: Preparing Bread.

THE DEATHS OF SARAH AND ABRAHAM

(based on Genesis 23:1, 19 and 25:7-11)

Sarah lived to be 125 years old. When she died, Abraham bought some land and buried her in a cave there. Abraham lived to be 175 years old. When he died his sons, Isaac and Ishmael buried him in the cave where Sarah his wife had been buried. After the death of Abraham, God's blessing was with his son Isaac.

Hebron

Tradition identifies Hebron as the burial place of Sarah and Abraham. This is why Hebron is a holy place for the Jewish people. Muslims also honour Abraham. They call him El Khalil, which means 'friend of God'.

Genesis

Esau and Jacob (based on Genesis 25:20-27)

Isaac was forty years old when he married Rebecca.

Isaac and Rebecca prayed to God that they would have children. Rebecca worried that she would not be able to have a child.

God answered their prayers and Rebecca had twins. The first to be born they called Esau. When the second twin was born, they called him Jacob.

When Esau grew up, he became a skilled hunter who loved the open countryside.

Jacob was a quiet man who preferred to stay at home around the tents.

Isaac loved Esau best because he liked to eat whatever Esau caught.

Rebecca loved Jacob most.

The Children of Israel (based on Genesis 35:9-15, 23-26)

God blessed Jacob. God gave him the name Israel.

Jacob had twelve sons:

Reuben, Simeon, Levi, Judah, Issachar, Zebulon, Joseph, Benjamin, Dan, Naphtali, Gad and Asher.

These twelve sons are regarded as the fathers of the twelve tribes of Israel. In the Bible, the People of God are often called 'children of Israel'.

Genesis

Jacob and his sons were shepherds and farmers.

A Berber woman weaver. Many patterns have been handed down from mother to daughter for hundreds of years.

JOSEPH (based on Genesis 37:3, 4, 12, 13, 18-28, 31-33)

Israel loved Joseph more than all his other sons. He had a beautiful coat made for him. It was long and had full sleeves. Joseph's brothers hated him because he was their father's favourite. They hardly ever spoke a friendly word to him.

One day, when his brothers were out in Schechem looking after the sheep, Israel said to Joseph, "Go and see how your brothers are and how the sheep are doing, then come back and tell me."

When his brothers saw Joseph coming, they planned to kill him. Reuben tried to save him. "Let's not hurt him. Let's just throw him down this well."

They ripped off his beautiful long robe with the full sleeves and threw him down the well, which was dry. Then they sat down to eat.

While they were eating, some merchants came by on their way to Egypt. Judah said, "Why don't we sell Joseph to these merchants instead of leaving him here in this well to die?"

So they pulled Joseph out of the well and sold him for twenty pieces of silver. The merchants took Joseph to Egypt.

Joseph's brothers took his beautiful robe, dipped it in the blood of a goat, which they had killed, and had it taken to their father. When Jacob saw the robe, he knew that it was Joseph's and he wept for his son.

Genesis

JOSEPH IN EGYPT (based on Genesis 39:1-4 and 41:38-48, 57)

When the merchants arrived in Egypt, they sold Joseph to Potiphar, the captain of the palace guard. Potiphar soon recognised that God was with Joseph. He was so pleased with everything that Joseph did that he put him in charge of his house.

The Pharaoh got to know how clever and hard-working Joseph was and made him governor of Egypt. Joseph was thirty years old. Pharaoh took a ring from his own finger and put it on Joseph's. He dressed him in fine robes made from linen and put a gold chain around Joseph's neck. He said, "I am Pharaoh, and I say – no one in Egypt shall so much as move a hand or foot without your permission."

A tomb painting showing corn crops and officials

Joseph arranged for the storage of food when the harvests were good. When a great famine came, there was food in Egypt for everyone, and people began to come from all the countries around where the famine was terrible.

Family farm today.

Drought.

Genesis

The Nile Delta and the Sinai Peninsula.

TOGETHER AGAIN (based on Genesis 42-47)

Jacob heard about the food supplies in Egypt and sent his sons to see what they could get, but he would not let Benjamin, his youngest son, leave him.

When the brothers arrived in Egypt, Joseph knew them, but they did not recognise him. He acted as if he did not know them. He demanded that they go and fetch Benjamin and kept Simeon as a hostage.

When they came back with Benjamin, Joseph set them another test. His servants planted a silver cup in Benjamin's sack of corn. Joseph ordered their sacks searched, and when the cup was found said they had stolen it. He threatened to keep Benjamin as his slave. His brothers begged him to keep any one of them and let Benjamin go free. Then Joseph said, "I am your brother, Joseph."

The brothers were very happy to see Joseph alive and to know that he had forgiven them. Israel and all his family came to Egypt to live, and the Pharaoh welcomed them. They settled down with their families and their flocks of sheep.

The children of Israel and their descendants lived in Egypt for centuries, up until the time of Moses.

Genesis 17

EXODUS

For God's People the road to freedom led through the desert.

God takes care of the chosen people. God leads them out of Egypt to a land of their own and gives them commandments.

Exodus

TROUBLE IN EGYPT (based on Exodus 1: 8-14)

Now a new Pharaoh, who knew nothing about Joseph, became the ruler of Egypt.

"There are so many Israelites living here now," he said to the Egyptians, "and they are stronger than us. We must do something in case war breaks out and they join the enemy to fight against us."

So the Egyptians made slaves of the Israelites and set them to work on their building projects and in their fields. They did all the hard, and heavy work and their lives became more and more miserable.

Pyramids in Egypt today.

Exodus

GOD CHOOSES MOSES (based on Exodus 3:1-8)

Moses was looking after his father-in-law's sheep. He led them through the desert and came to a holy mountain, Mount Sinai. There he saw a bush. It seemed to be on fire, burning brightly, but not burning up.

"How strange," Moses thought. "Why isn't the bush burning up? I must go and see this strange sight."

As he approached the bush, he heard God speak to him. "Moses," God called.

"Yes, Lord," Moses said, "I am here."

"Moses, do not come any closer. You are standing on holy ground. Take off your sandals. I am your God, the God of your ancestors, of Abraham, of Isaac and of Jacob."

Moses was afraid; he hid his face in his hands.

God spoke again. "I have seen how my people have been suffering dreadfully as slaves in Egypt. I have heard their prayers that they might be saved. I am going to rescue them from the Egyptians and bring them to a new and wonderful land. I am sending you. You are to go to Pharaoh so that you can lead my people out of Egypt."

Moses pleaded with God. "Who am I? How can I possibly do this?"

"I shall be with you," God said. "When you have led the people out of Egypt, you will come to worship on this holy mountain."

MOSES

Moses was born in Egypt at a time when God's People were slaves, and all boy babies born to Israelite families were taken away at birth. Moses' mother hid him in a basket among the reeds on the riverbank. The Pharaoh's daughter found him there and brought him up herself. When he grew up, he found out that he was an Israelite and soon after that he left Egypt and joined a family of nomads in the desert. These wandering people had flocks of sheep and goats, and so Moses became a shepherd.

THE ESCAPE TO FREEDOM

The story of how God saved them and led them to freedom is a very important story for the Chosen People.

LET MY PEOPLE GO (based on Exodus 4:28-31, 5:6-9; 10:28; 12:31,32)

Moses went back to Egypt. He told Aaron his brother everything that God had said to him. Then they gathered the leaders of the Israelites together and told them what had happened. The people rejoiced because God had seen how cruelly they were treated. They bowed down and worshipped God. Then Moses and Aaron went to Pharaoh and said, "The God of Israel says, 'Let my people go'."

Pharaoh refused and made the Israelites work even harder. God spoke to Moses again, "Go and tell Pharaoh that he must let the Israelites leave Egypt."

Pharaoh was stubborn, and time and again refused to let the Israelites depart, but God was with the Israelites, and eventually Pharaoh agreed to let them go. Pharaoh said to Moses and Aaron, "Go, you and your people. Go and worship your God. Take your sheep, goats and cattle with you, and pray for a blessing for me."

A refugee camp today. Many people still suffer the loss of their homes.

Exodus

THE PASSOVER MEAL (based on Exodus 12:3,4,8,11,14)

Before leaving, they ate a special meal together, to celebrate God's love for them. It is called 'Passover'. God gave them some instructions about the meal.

Each family must take one animal from the flock.

If your family is too small to eat all the meat, then share it with your next-door neighbours.

The animal can either be a sheep or a goat.

Make sure it's roasted over a fire so that it's well cooked!

You must eat it with unleavened bread and bitter herbs.

If there's anything left over, burn it.

This is how you must eat it:
with a belt around your waist,
your sandals on your feet,
and your staff in your hand.

You must be dressed for a journey.

You won't have time to sit down to eat the meal.

You must eat it quickly.

It is a Passover meal.

You must celebrate this day each year,
as a holy day, to remember and honour me
for all time.

The story of the escape to freedom is told by Jewish families each year at Passover.

Exodus

A Prayer for the People (based on Psalm 80:8-17)

Remember God; you brought a vine out of Egypt.

You cleared space around it.

Nothing and no one could prevent it from flourishing.

It took root and filled the whole country.

It grew so high that it covered mountains
with the shade of its leaves.

It wound its branches around the magnificent cedar trees.

It grew so wide that it reached
from the sea to the river Euphrates.

Why have you broken down the fences that protected it?

Now anyone can steal its fruit.

The wild pigs can tear it to pieces,
and fierce animals can eat it all.

Please, God of all people, have pity on us.

Look on us from heaven. Look at this vine. Be with it.

Protect what you have taken the trouble to plant.

They have thrown it on the fire as though it was worthless.

But if you give them only one cross look
they will be overcome.

Please, Lord, protect those who are close to you,
those who have been given power by you.

We will never forget you again.

Give us life, and we will call upon your name.

> Why do you think the writer says God's People are like a vine?
>
> What other picture images might you use?

Exodus

JOURNEY TO THE PROMISED LAND

After Moses had led them from slavery in Egypt, the Israelites wandered in the desert for many years. Nearly always they rejoiced in their freedom. Sometimes they suffered hardships. Sometimes even hunger and thirst, but always God provided for them in spite of their grumbles.

WATER TO DRINK (based on Exodus 15:22-25, 27)

Moses led his people from their camp at the Sea of Reeds and through the desert into the wilderness of Shur. They travelled for three days without water. Eventually, they found water at a place called Marah, meaning bitter, and indeed the water there was so bitter they could not drink it. The people grumbled at Moses. "What are we to drink?" they said. Moses prayed to God. God answered his prayer. Moses recognised a special kind of wood. When he placed it in the water, it became sweet. After quenching their thirst, the people were able to travel to Elim. There they found twelve springs of water, and seventy palm trees. Here they pitched their camp beside the waters.

FOOD TO EAT (based on Exodus 16:13-16)

The whole Israelite community set out from Elim, and on the fifteenth day of the second month after they had left Egypt, they came to the desert of Sin, which is between Elim and Sinai. There in the desert, they complained to Moses, "We wish that God had let us die in Egypt. There we could at least sit down and eat meat and as much food as we wanted. But you have brought us out into this desert to starve us all to death."

The Lord answered saying to Moses: "Now I am going to make bread rain down from the sky for all of you. The people must go out every day and gather enough for that day." That evening, quails flew in and covered the camp. Next morning there was dew all over the camp and when the dew evaporated there was something thin and flaky on the surface of the desert. It was as delicate as frost. When the Israelites saw it, they didn't know what it was and asked each other, "What is it?" Moses said to them, "This is the food that the Lord has given you to eat. The Lord has commanded that each of you is to gather as much of it as you need each day, two litres for each member of your household."

Manna is Hebrew for 'What is it?' Insects living in the tamarisk trees in Sinai form an edible substance, which is gathered for food.

Quails migrate from Europe in September. Tired by their long journey across the Mediterranean they land in large numbers in Sinai.

The wood of a desert shrub takes away the bitterness of desert water.

A waterfall in the desert.

A tamarisk tree in flower.

Quails feeding.

Exodus

GOD'S COMMANDMENTS (based on Exodus 20:8-11)

The Israelites were already two hundred miles from Egypt when they reached **Mount Sinai** and camped there. Moses ordered the people not to climb the mountain's slopes because it was a holy mountain. He was going to climb the mountain, and he asked them to pray that God would teach them the laws that would bind them together as a people. He was away for a long time, praying and talking with God. Then he returned to the people. Moses told them God's Laws, the Ten Commandments and they accepted them as God's gift and the rules for a new way of life.

St Catherine's monastery at the foot of Mount Sinai

Mount Sinai

Sinai is one mountain peak in the rocky desert to the north of the Red Sea. It is a holy place for Jews and Christians because the Bible tells us that it was here that Moses received the ten commandments: Exodus 20:1-20; Deuteronomy 5: 6-23. It was here that the Jewish refugees from Egypt became God's people and promised to be faithful to God's Law.

Today, there is a monastery at the foot of Mt Sinai. It has one of the oldest libraries in the world. It is a steep climb to the top of the mountain, but many people make the climb to look out at the view that Moses would have seen.

Exodus

Remember the Sabbath day, a day to rest.
Make it a holy day.
For six days during the week, you work very hard.
The seventh day is a Sabbath, a day for God.
On that day you must do no work.
Neither must your son or your daughter
nor anyone else in your house.
For when God made the heavens
and the earth and all that is in them,
God worked hard for six days,
but on the seventh day, God rested.
This is why God has blessed the seventh day,
the Sabbath, and made it holy.

Honour and respect your father and mother.
Do not kill.
Do not be unfaithful.
Do not steal.
Do not tell lies against your neighbour.
Do not become eaten up with greed for
what you do not have.
(based on Deuteronomy 5:12-21)

Time to Think
Do not kill.
Life is God's holy gift.
Do not be unfaithful.
Loving is part of God's plan.
Do not steal.
*Respect other people's possessions
and protect the rights of the poor.*
Do not tell lies against your neighbour.
*Truth reflects God's faithfulness and
goodness.*
Do not become eaten up with greed for
what you do not have.
It will rob you of the joy of living.

Exodus

LEVITICUS & DEUTERONOMY

LEVITICUS

This book contains teachings of a group of priests. It has a lot of advice about worship and the behaviour expected from God's people. The key words in this book are: 'Love your neighbour as yourself'.

"Listen Israel; our God is the one and only God. You must love your God with all your heart, with all your soul, with all your strength."

These words are the opening words of the Shema, a special prayer for Jewish people. When Jesus was asked which was the greatest commandment, he quoted these words from Deuteronomy and Leviticus and said that they summed up God's law.

DEUTERONOMY

This book is written as if it were a collection of speeches or sermons given by Moses. Moses reminds the people that God loves them and has blessed them. They are to remember this and love and obey God so that they may have life and continue to be blessed by their God. The key words in this book are: 'Love the Lord your God with all your heart, with all your soul and with all your strength'.

Love your neighbour as yourself

Leviticus & Deuteronomy

TELL YOUR CHILDREN (based on Deuteronomy 6:4-9)

Listen Israel, our God is the one and only God.

You must love your God with all your heart, with all your soul, with all your strength.

Keep these words always in your heart.

Tell them to your children and keep on telling them.

Tell them when you are sitting at home; when you are out and about; when you are lying down, and when you are standing up.

A SONG OF THE JOURNEY (based on Deuteronomy 32:10-14)

God found us in the desert,
Wandering in that lonely, windy place.
God cared for us and kept us safe.

Just like an eagle guarding its nest
or teaching its young to fly,
God spread out wings to hold us,
to catch us if we fell.

God alone was our guide.
God was the one who led us.
God gave the highlands to us.

God fed us with wild honey found among the rocks there
and oil from the olive trees,
which grew in hard and stony ground.
God gave us what grew in the fields:
the finest of wheat for our bread
and the sweetest of grapes for our wine;
the best of sheep and goats,
cows that gave plenty of milk.

Leviticus & Deuteronomy

CARE FOR OTHERS (based on Leviticus 19:9-10)

When harvest time comes do not cut the crops to the very
edges of the fields and do not return to collect the scraps that are left.

You must not go back through your vineyard
to gather the grapes that you missed.

You must not pick up those which have fallen.

Leave them for poor people and strangers who are hungry.

I am your God.

AND GOD SAID (based on Leviticus 26:3-5)

"I want you to live your life
according to the laws that I have given you.

Keep to my rules and put them into practice.

I, for my part, will do this:

I will send the rain pouring down from the heavens
at just the right time.

Earth will soak up the rain,
and the trees and the crops will flourish.

You will have plenty to eat and to drink.

You will have rich wine
because the vines will bear many grapes.

If you keep my rules, you will have bread to eat,
and you will live secure on your land."

How might the world be different if people kept God's laws?

What rules help you...

- at home?
- at school?
- at church?
- around the neighbourhood?

Leviticus & Deuteronomy

All over the world harvest time means work to be done and produce to share. Harvesting wheat, dates, honey, rice and olives.

Leviticus & Deuteronomy

SAMUEL & KINGS

After Moses had died, God chose Joshua to lead the Israelites into the land promised to them. "My servant Moses is now dead," God said to Joshua, "Go now, you and all my people. Cross the River Jordan into the land that I am giving to you. Everywhere you walk shall be yours. All the land from the desert and the Lebanon, to the great river, the Euphrates, and as far as the great sea is to be yours."

God continued to give the Israelites leaders to guide them. They helped them to defend the land God had given them when their enemies tried to invade it. These leaders were called Judges.

The books of Samuel and Kings tell the history of God's people, of the judges and kings of Israel and how many tribes were brought together around one king and one capital city Jerusalem.

Samuel was the last of the great judges.

God continued to give the Israelites leaders to guide them.

Samuel & Kings

The Birth of Samuel (based on Samuel 1:9-28)

Hannah longed for a baby. She prayed trustfully, telling God of all her hopes for a child. Time went by, and Hannah prayed more fervently every day.

A Jewish mother & child.

The time came to celebrate a special feast, and she and her husband travelled to Shiloh for the festivities. The priest at Shiloh was a kindly old man called Eli. When he saw Hannah deep in prayer, he thought there was something wrong and went over to ask her. She told him how much she longed for a baby and how long and hard she had prayed to God. Eli encouraged her not to give up hoping and praying. "God loves everyone," he reminded her.

At last Hannah did have a baby. She called him Samuel. She took him to the house of the Lord at Shiloh and went to Eli, the priest.

"Do you remember me?" she asked. "I am the woman you saw praying to the Lord. I asked for this child, and God has given me what I asked for. So now I am dedicating him to the Lord. As long as he lives, he will be holy to the Lord."

Then, together Hannah and Eli praised God for Samuel.

She brought Samuel up knowing that she would give him back to God to serve him.

Hannah's Prayer

God has filled my heart with joy.
I am so happy.
God has done great things for me.
I am so happy
for God has helped me.
God's name is holy.
There is no one like God.
God is so very good.
God is always near.
(based on 1 Samuel 2:1-10)

Samuel & Kings

THE CALL OF SAMUEL (based on Samuel 2:11; 3:3-10)

When Samuel was old enough, he went to Shiloh to stay with Eli and grew up in the service of God.

One night when Samuel was asleep, he heard someone calling him. He jumped up quickly and ran to Eli. "Here I am," he said.

Eli answered, "I did not call you; go back to bed."

Samuel did as Eli said. Then he heard someone calling him again. So he got up, went to Eli and said, "You called me; here I am."

Eli said again, "I did not call you; go back to bed."

Samuel heard someone calling him a third time. He got up, went to Eli and said again, "You called me; here I am."

Eli realised that it was God who was calling Samuel. This time, he said, "Go back to bed. If you hear the voice again, say, 'Speak Lord, I am listening'." So Samuel went back to bed. When the voice called again, 'Samuel, Samuel,' he answered, "Speak Lord I am listening."

GOD'S PROPHET (based on 1 Samuel 3:19-21 and 1 Samuel 8:1-6, 10, 22)

As Samuel grew up, God was always close to him, and Samuel always listened to God's word. He became God's prophet, and the people listened to what he had to say.

When Samuel grew old, he made his sons Judges in Israel. Samuel's sons did not follow his example. They did not listen to God's word. The people asked Samuel to give them a king. "Look," they said, "you are old, and your sons do not follow your example. So give us a king to rule us, like the other nations."

Samuel listened to all they had to say and then prayed to God. God said to Samuel, "Do as they ask and give them a king."

THE FIRST KING (based on 1 Samuel 10:1 and 1 Samuel 15:10, 24; 16:1)

God chose Saul to be the first king of Israel. Samuel took some oil and poured it on Saul's head. He kissed him and said, "God has anointed you as king of God's people Israel."

But Saul did not listen to God's word. He was afraid of the people and did what they wanted, not what God wanted. God was sorry that he had made Saul king. God sent Samuel to find a new king for Israel.

DAVID IS CHOSEN (based on 1 Samuel 16:4-13)

Samuel went to Bethlehem. A man named Jesse, who had eight sons, lived there.

When he saw Eliab, the eldest of the sons, Samuel thought that he must be the one God had chosen. God said to Samuel, "Take no notice of his height. I have not chosen him. I do not see as human beings see. They look at appearances; I look at the heart."

Jesse then called Abinadab, but God had not chosen him. Next, he called Shammah, but God had not chosen him either. Jesse presented seven of his sons to Samuel.

Samuel said to Jesse, "God has not chosen any of these. Are they all the sons you have?"

Jesse answered, "There is one left, the youngest; He is looking after the sheep."

Samuel asked Jesse to send for him. When David arrived, Samuel took some oil and anointed him in front of his brothers. God blessed David and was close to him.

The People of God remember David as a beloved king and leader. This psalm thanks God for the King.

(based on Psalm 21)

Oh God, our King rejoices in your power!
You have always helped him.
You have given him great joy.
You have given him all that his heart wants.

You have blessed him with the best of blessings;
a crown of gold is on his head.
He asked for a long life, and you gave it to him.
You have given him glory.

You have helped him.
You have given him splendour and majesty.
You have blessed him forever.
You are with him, and this brings him joy.
Because our King trusts you
he will rule in safety
and his enemies will never win.

Oh God, how great is your power!
We will sing and rejoice in your presence.

How did David find out what God wanted him to be?

How do you think he felt?

A shepherd in Palestine today.

Samuel & Kings

DAVID AND SOLOMON (based on 1 Kings 1:33,34,39)

When King David was an old man, he made his son Solomon king of Israel. Zadok the priest and Nathan the prophet anointed Solomon as king. They blew the trumpet, and all the people rejoiced and cried out, "Long live King Solomon."

DAVID'S ADVICE (based on 1 Kings 2:1-4, 10-12)

Just before he died, King David said to his son Solomon, "My life is coming to an end. Be strong and always do what God wants you to do. Obey the commandments God gave to Moses. If you do this, God will be with you always."

David died and was buried in the City of David. He had been king for forty years.

Solomon then sat on the throne of David and ruled with power and wisdom.

SOLOMON'S PRAYER FOR WISDOM (based on 1 Kings 3:7-12)

"O Lord you have made me king, but I am only a young man, and I do not know how to rule. Here I am among the people you have chosen to be your own, a people so great it cannot be counted. Make me truly wise. Give me, your servant, a heart which understands the difference between good and evil, for without this I cannot govern your people."

God was pleased with Solomon's prayer. God said to Solomon, "Since you have asked for the wisdom to rule well and not for a long life for yourself, or for riches, or for the death of your enemies, I will give it to you right here and now. I will give you a wiser and more understanding heart than anyone has ever had."

SOLOMON'S REIGN (based on 1 Kings 4:29-34)

Solomon was the wisest of kings. His fame spread to all the neighbouring countries. He composed three hundred proverbs and more than a thousand songs. His knowledge could not be measured. He knew all about the plants and trees, the animals and birds, the reptiles and fish. People from all the neighbouring countries came to listen to Solomon's wisdom.

Samuel & Kings

King David is honoured at this place called King David's tomb.

The Book of Ruth

This book tells the story of Ruth the great-grandmother of David. Ruth came from Moab. She married an Israelite called Chilion, who had come with his parents, Elimelech and Naomi, and his brother Mahlon, to live in Moab when there was a famine in Israel. After her husband and two sons died Naomi decided to return to her own people in the land of Judah.

Let me go with you (based on Ruth 1:2-7,16,17)

Ruth said to Naomi, "Let me go with you. Wherever you go, I will go with you. Wherever you live, I will too. Your people shall be my people, and your God shall be my God".

Ruth's family (based on Ruth 2: 2; 4:13,17)

So Ruth went with Naomi to Bethlehem, in the land of Judah. There she married Boaz, a relative of Naomi. God blessed her, and she had a son who was called Obed. Obed was the father of Jesse, who was the father of David.

Samuel & Kings

THE TEMPLE (based on 1Kings 5:16-19,20,25,27,29,30,31; 6: 29,30; 7:3)

Solomon's father David was not able to build a temple for the worship of God because he was always busy defending his people from their enemies.

God gave Solomon peace with his neighbours. He had no enemies, and the land was not in danger of attack. So Solomon decided to build a temple for God. He had juniper, wild olive trees and cedars from Lebanon cut down and special stones quarried and dressed for the building of the Temple. He hired thirty thousand labourers, seventy thousand porters and eighty thousand quarrymen, as well as men to supervise them. All around the temple he had winged creatures, palm trees and rosettes carved. He had both these and the floor of the temple overlaid with gold. It took seven years to build the temple, and it was completed exactly as Solomon had designed it.

THE TEMPLE MOUNT IN JERUSALEM

David wanted very much to build a Temple, a holy place for the Jewish people's greatest treasure, the Ark of the Covenant. The Ark had been built at the time of Moses. It was a box of Acacia wood. In it was kept God's Law, the sign that God was with the chosen people. It was David's son, Solomon who saw to the building of the Temple. It was magnificent, taking seven years to complete. All the work was done by hand by skilled craftsmen.

The Romans destroyed it in 70A.D. Today you can see the great stone blocks that were the foundations of Solomon's Temple at a place called the wailing wall.

SOLOMON'S PRAYER FOR HIS PEOPLE

(based on 1Kings 8:30,57-59)

God of Israel,

Whenever your people pray in this place, listen to our prayer and forgive us.

Be with us always; never abandon us.

Turn our hearts towards you,
so that we may always follow your ways and keep your commandments.

Be with us always night and day.

Samuel & Kings

A model of Jerusalem at the time of King Solomon.

A model of Solomon's Temple.

Praying at The Western Wall.

Samuel & Kings

PSALMS

It is good to talk with God in every situation. Psalms are prayers written for every situation: joy, sadness, fear, doubt, and trust. This book is a collection of 150 psalms.

Some of the psalms are joyful praise for God; some give thanks for all God's goodness to us; some say sorry for wrong done; others ask for all that people need in order to live, to love and to serve God. Some describe what pleases God.

All good Jews tried to go to Jerusalem each year for the three great feast days. Journeys in those days had to be made on foot or riding on a donkey, so it took almost a week. Often there were robbers about, so the pilgrims travelled in large groups for safety. The men travelled together, and the women kept together too. The children would run from group to group, sometimes with the men, sometimes with the women.

As they travelled along, they often sang to keep themselves cheerful and pass the time, but each day, at particular times, they sang their prayers in preparation for the feast they were going to celebrate. There were particular psalms for each stage of the journey. They looked forward to the moment when they would catch sight of the beautiful Temple as they came over the hills. One psalm expressed the great joy of the pilgrims actually standing inside the Temple in God's presence:

I rejoiced when I heard them say: 'Let us go to God's house'.

And now our feet are standing within your gates, O Jerusalem.

The Jewish people and Christians still sing these prayers today.

Psalms

Just like a shepherd.

Pilgrimage Psalms pp42-43
Psalms 84, 118, 122

Prayers for Help pp44-45
Psalms 6, 22, 44, 130

Psalms of Trust in God's Love pp46-47
Psalms 23, 46, 136, 146

Creation Psalms pp48-51
Psalms 49, 65, 98, 104, 139

Psalm of Thanks and Praise p52
Psalm 100

Who loves to be happy?

I am feeling very unhappy.

Psalms 41

PILGRIMAGE PSALMS

Dear God, I long to be in your beautiful Temple.
My whole being sings for joy to you.
Sparrows looking for a home are safe in your house.
Swallows build their nests
and feed their young beside your altars.

Those who live in your temple are so happy
they can praise you all day long.
Pilgrims travel through deep valleys
and climb steep hills
to visit your special place.

One day spent in the Temple courtyards
is better than a thousand spent anywhere else!
It is good to put our trust in you.
Dear God, you keep us safe from harm.

(based on Psalm 84)

I was full of joy when they said to me,
Let's go up to God's house.
And now, at last, we are standing
inside the gates of Jerusalem.

Jerusalem is a great city, the city of peace.
The people of Israel come here
to give thanks to God.

Pray for the peace of Jerusalem.
Pray for peace in your homes.
Pray for peace among yourselves.
Pray for peace in your land.

For love of my brothers and sisters,
I will say 'Peace be with you'.
For love of the house of God,
I will pray for your good.

(based on Psalm 122:1-9)

Bar Mitzvah procession at the Western Wall in Jerusalem.

Psalms

Pilgrims on the road in Spain.

Alleluia
Give thanks to God for God is good.

God's love is great and never ends.

Open the temple gates for me.
I will go in and give thanks to God.
Give thanks to God for God is good.

God's love is great and never ends.

This is God's gate
Where those who love God enter.
Give thanks to God for God is good.

God's love is great and never ends.

May God bless everyone
who comes to give thanks and praise.
Give thanks to God for God is good.

God's love is great and never ends.

Walk in procession around the altar.
Wave your branches high.
Give thanks to God for God is good.

God's love is great and never ends.
Alleluia.

(based on Psalm 118:19-20,26-29)

Pilgrims gather in St Peter's Square for the Pope's midday blessing.

Psalms

Prayers for help

Please, God,
do not be angry with me.
Look on me kindly.
I am feeling very unhappy.

Help me, because I know you love me.
I am worn out with moaning and groaning.
Every night I cry myself to sleep.
My eyes are red and sore; I cry so much.

God has heard me crying.
God has listened to me.
I know my God will help me.

(based on Psalm 6. A psalm of David. vv.1-4, 8-9)

I am feeling dreadful!
I call to you my God.
Hear my call. Listen to my cry for help.
If you kept a list of our sins,
we would be lost.

But you forgive us, and we are amazed by you.
I am waiting for your help O God.
I am longing for your help to come,
even more than a night-watchman is longing,
for the night to be over and the dawn to break.

(based on Psalm 130:1-6)

Wake up, God! Why are you asleep?
Wake up, God!
Have you forgotten us?
Wake up, God!
Why are you hiding from us?

Wake up, God!
Do you not know how wretched we feel?
Wake up, God!
Do you not know that we feel crushed?
Wake up, God!

Come on, God! God! Wake up!
We know you won't forget us.
We know how much you love us.

(based on Psalm 44 a traditional psalm vv. 23-26)

Psalms

War Orphans in Sudan.

My God, my God, why have you left me all alone?
I have cried to you for help, but no help comes.
All day long I call to you, my God,
but you do not answer me.
All night long I cry to you, but I get no rest.

You were there when I was born,
when I was a baby you kept me safe.
I have trusted in you ever since I was a little child.
You have always been there for me;
do not stay away from me now I am in trouble.
There is no one to help me, my strength is gone.
I am aching all over; my heart is broken,
my throat is parched.
My tongue sticks to the roof of my mouth.
My God, don't leave me all alone.

Come quickly to my help.
I feel so helpless.
I will tell everyone I meet all about you.
I will tell them all that you have done for me.

God does not forget me when I am poor and in trouble.
God does not ignore me.
God does not turn away from me.
God answers me when I cry for help.
I praise you for what you do for me.
Praise God, everyone!

(based on Psalm 22: 1-2, 9-11, 14-15, 19, 22-25)

Psalm 22 In the gospels of Matthew and Luke, Jesus cries out to God in the opening words of this psalm. Have you noticed how the psalm changes from a cry of help to confidence in God's love?

War can make children orphans and separate them without news of their loved ones.

Psalms

TRUST IN GOD'S LOVE

God cares for me
just like a shepherd cares for his sheep.
I have all that I need.
God, you give me green meadows
where I can lie down.
You lead me to tranquil streams of fresh water
where I find new strength.
You guide me along safe paths.
You are true to your name.

Even if I should walk in deep darkness,
I would not be afraid.
For you would be close to me,
protecting me from harm.

You prepare a great feast for me.
You welcome me
and anoint my forehead with oil.
You fill my cup to overflowing.

I am sure your love and goodness
will be with me every day of my life.
Your house will be my home for ever and ever.

(based on Psalm 23)

God is always there for me:
Always ready to help me when I am in trouble.
Even when there are earthquakes, storms and floods
I need not be afraid.

God is always with me, sheltering me from harm.

God is with me all day.
My world is in uproar, my life is falling apart,
but God comes to my rescue, nothing can harm me.

God is always with me, sheltering me from harm.

Come and look at the wonders of God,
the marvellous work God has done on earth.
"Stop fighting," God says,
"Be still and know that I am God."

God is always with me, sheltering me from harm.

(A Psalm of David. Based on
Psalm 46:1,2,9,11,14,15, 19,22-24)

Psalms

Give thanks to our God for God is so good.
Give thanks to our great God
for love that lasts forever.
Give thanks to our strong God
for love, that is never ending.

Our God does wonderful works.
Our God is so very wise.
Our God made the vast heavens.
Our God built the earth and the deep seas.
God made the sun and the moon:
the sun to shine all the day;
the moon and the stars
to shine through the night.

God is always with us.
God never forgets us.
God takes such great care of us.
Give thanks to our God!
Our God is so good!

(based on Psalm 136:1,5,9,23-26)

Come, my children. Listen to me.
Who loves to be happy all the time?
Who enjoys having good times together?
Well – so does God!

Be careful about what you say.
Don't say anything to hurt anyone.
Don't tell a lie.
Keep away from what is wrong.

Always do what is right and good.
Be the one to bring peace.
Remember!

God cares for you.

God knows what you want.

God listens.

(based on Psalm 34:11-15)

Come Lord, and save us!

God, you are always faithful,
always kind to those who are harshly treated.
You give food to those who are hungry.
You set free those who are imprisoned.

Come Lord and save us!

You give sight to those who are blind.
You lift the spirits of those who are sad.
You protect the stranger.
You help the orphan and the widow.

Come Lord and save us!

(based on Psalm 146: 7-9)

Psalms

CREATION PSALMS

In this psalm, David is thanking God for his beginning in his mother's womb. He thanks God for being there creating him and for remaining with him all through his life.

Great and wonderful creator God!
I thank you, and I praise you
for creating wonderful me!

Whilst I was in my mother's womb
You loved me, and you knew me.
You watched me growing and moving.
You loved me, and you knew me.

And now, Creator God, you still watch me.
You love me, and you know me.
Even before I speak, you know my words.
You love me, and you know me.

If I were to climb the highest mountain,
You would be there.
If I swam and swam until I could swim no more
You would be there,
your hand ready to hold me and guide me.
You are always there.

Great and wonderful Creator God!
I thank you, and I praise you
for creating wonderful me.

Your thoughts and dreams for me
are as many as the stars in heaven
and grains of sand on the seashore.
I think You are just WONDERFUL!
Great and wonderful Creator God
I thank you, and I praise you!

(based on Psalm 139:13-15, 8-10, 17-18)

Psalms

O sing to the Lord a new song!
Sing to the Lord all the earth.
Sing to the Lord all people on earth.
Sing of God's goodness and wonderful deeds.

Let the sky and the land be happy.
Let the deep sea shout out loud.
Let everything in the sea be glad.

Let the fields sing out for joy.
Let everything that grows be cheerful.
Let trees of the wood dance and sing.
God comes to visit the world.
God comes to bring justice to all people.

(based on Psalm 96: 1,7,11-13)

Psalms

Sing for joy to God all the earth!
Praise God with songs and shouts of happiness.
Play music on the harp.
Blow the trumpet, sound the horn.
Acclaim the presence of our God.

Let the sea roar;
all creatures in it thunder praise.
Let the earth sing
and all who live in it shout for joy.

Let the rivers clap their hands
and the hills sing together in delight
as God draws near.
God comes to bring justice and fairness to the world.

(based on Psalm 98 a traditional psalm vv. 4-9)

The whole world sings for joy,
God, how good you are.

You care for our land with loving-kindness.
You send gentle rain so that seeds begin to grow.
You send spring sunshine to welcome fresh new shoots.
The wheat will grow strong and straight.
The harvest will be ready
and fruits all ripe to eat.

The whole world sings for joy,
How good you are God!

(based on Psalm 65:10-14)

Psalms

My God, how great you are!
You give new life to the world.

The springs are full of water;
the rivers run down the mountains;
animals have plenty to drink;
wild donkeys are thirsty no more.
The birds up in the trees
build their nests and sing their songs.

You pour down life-giving rain;
the grass begins to grow;
crops spring up;
people have plenty to eat:
wine to gladden their hearts;
oil to make their faces glow.

All creation is blessed:
the trees grow tall;
the birds make their nests,
the storks build homes in the highest trees;
the wild goats enjoy the mountains;
the rabbits hide in the cliffs.

You made the moon to mark the seasons;
the sun knows when to set.
Some animals come out only at night
to find the food that you provide.
The sun rises, and they go back to sleep.
Most people work in the day
from morning light until evening dusk.

What wonders you do in the world.
They are far too many to count.
The world is full of your creatures.
And indeed so are the seas.
The ocean holds countless fish;
great whales play in it;
fine ships pass over the waves.

They all depend on you
to feed them when they need it.
You provide the food they gather;
your open hand gives them their fill.
Without you, they would die.

My God how great you are!
You give new life to the world.
Glory to you forever!

**(based on
Psalm 104:10-30)**

Psalms 51

Praise and Thanksgiving

Come, everyone, sing to God.
Joyfully sing to God.
Sing cheerful songs!

Come, everyone, sing to God.
We are glad to praise our God.
The God who made us all.
We belong together.
Come, everyone, sing to God.
Give God thanks and praise
Bless God's holy name.

Come, everyone, sing to God.
God's love is forever, unending;
God is with us always.

Come, everyone, sing to God.

(based on Psalm 100:1-5)

Psalms

WISDOM

The Wisdom books collect proverbs and the thoughts of people who have spent time thinking long and deeply about life and God and people.

PROVERBS

This book contains a collection of teachings or wise sayings taken from the writings of the wise men of Israel. Many of them are thought to be the work of Solomon. Another name for a wise man is a 'sage'. Solomon was one of the greatest of all the sages of Israel.

SONG OF SONGS

A love song, chosen to tell us how much God loves us, how tenderly and warmly.

ECCLESIASTES

This book collects the thoughts of 'the Preacher' someone who shares his thoughts about the mystery of life and ways of God with the people.

ECCLESIASTICUS

A wise man called Ben Sira wrote this to remind us that God will teach anyone how to be wise whenever they ask.

Thinking long and deeply about life and God and people.

Wisdom

LEARN FROM THE ANT (based on Proverbs 6: 6-11)

If you are a lazy bones,
then watch the ant.

No one tells her what to do.

No one supervises her,
yet she works hard the whole summer long.

She stores up food in preparation for winter.

Don't just sit around doing nothing.

If you do, you will have nothing
and be a nothing.

Ant at work

WISE SAYINGS

A fire goes out when there is no more wood.

A quarrel comes to an end when there are no more malicious words.
(based on Proverbs 26: 20)

Fools think that they are right; sensible people take advice.
(based on Proverbs 12:15)

Sensible people can spot trouble coming.

Silly people walk straight into it and are sorry when it is too late.
(based on Proverbs 22: 3)

Gossips cannot keep secrets.

Stay away from people who talk too much.
(based on Proverbs 20: 19)

LOOK AND SEE

(based on Song of Songs 2:11-13)

After winter's sleep, everything wakes up.

Flowers pop up; leaves burst open;
birds sing; the sun shines.

Come with me.

Look, the winter is over,
the rains have stopped,
the birds are singing,
the trees are growing.

Come with me
and smell the flowers.

Spring is here.

It is the time to be happy.

Wisdom

BEN SIRA'S PRAYER

(based on Ecclesiasticus 1:1,3,10)

God is very wise.
God made every grain of sand.
Can you count them all?
God can.

God made every drop of rain.
Can you count them all?
God can.

God made every day that has been, is,
and will ever be.
Can you count them all?
God can.

The sky is high above.
How high is the sky?
God knows.

The earth is so big.
How big is the earth?
God knows.

The sea is very deep.
How deep is the sea?
God knows.

God is very wise.

God shares what God knows with us.

This is God's gift to us.

REMEMBER GOD ALWAYS!

(based on Ecclesiastes 11:8-10)

It's good to be alive
when you are young and when you are old.

No matter how long you live,
there is always something you can find to be happy about.

Enjoy every minute of life, young people,
and remember God in everything you do.

Wisdom

A SEASON FOR EVERYTHING

(based on Ecclesiastes 3:1-8)

Everything happens in God's good time.
There is a time for everything;
a time for being born,
a time for dying;
a time for planting,
a time for gathering what was planted;
a time for killing,
a time for healing;
a time for knocking down,
a time for building;
a time for tears,
a time for laughter;
a time for mourning,
a time for dancing;
a time for hugging,
a time for not hugging;
a time for finding,
a time for losing;
a time for keeping,
a time for throwing away;
a time for tearing,
a time for mending;
a time for being silent
a time for speaking;
a time for loving,
a time for hating;
a time for war,
a time for peace.

Wisdom

You might like to write a poem or prayer or make a picture of special times in your life.

Wisdom

PROPHETS

The history of the People of God is a long story. There were good and bad times. There were good and bad kings. During the centuries of their history, God chose prophets to speak to the people, to encourage and advise them. The prophets reminded them of God's love and of the kind of people they were called to be. There are seventeen books named for prophets.

Each prophet shares something special about God.

ISAIAH

The writings of three different prophets are found under this one name. But all share concern about the holiness and faithfulness of God and the hope this gives.

JEREMIAH AND EZEKIEL

They were prophets when the kingdom was attacked, and the Temple destroyed. They went into exile with God's people. They used vivid images and symbols to encourage faith in God, obedience to God's commandments, and trust in God when things went wrong.

JOEL

Reminds us of God who is always ready to forgive.

HOSEA

Shares with us God's faithfulness and love that does not change despite people's faults and unfaithfulness.

AMOS

Challenges the people to care for the poor and those in need.

ZEPHANIAH

Calls people to look forward to the great things God will do to rescue them.

THE PROMISED ONE (based on Isaiah 7:14)

Listen now, House of David

God will give you a sign

It is this: a young woman

is pregnant and will have a son.

She will call him Emmanuel.

BRINGER OF PEACE

(based on Isaiah 9:1,5,6)

A long time ago

everything seemed sad and gloomy.

People felt as they were living in the dark.

But something happened.

It was as though a great light

brightened up their lives and made them happy.

For a child has been born for us.

A son is given to us.

And these are the names he has been given:

Strong Friend

Powerful God

Ever-loving Father

Bringer of Peace.

This child's kingdom will always be at peace.

He will rule as King David's successor

and from now till the end of time

he will rule justly and with fairness.

The Book of Isaiah contains some of the most beautiful poetry ever written. It uses 'picture-language', metaphor, to help people to see how much God loves and cares for them. Even when they were in the depths of sorrow and trouble, God will never abandon them.

Promised One

The titles given in this Isaiah passage indicate that the royal child will possess the wisdom of Solomon, David's courage and reverence for God and the great strength of faith of Moses and the patriarchs. The patriarchs are the leaders of the Israelite tribes and heads of prominent families who appear in Genesis from Adam to Joseph. (Isaiah 9:1,5,6)

Prophets

STRONG AND TRUE (based on Isaiah 11: 1-9)

Just as new shoots sometimes grow out of an old tree stump,
so will a new king come from the family of Jesse, father of King David.

The Spirit of God will be with him.

He will be wise and understand the meaning of life.

He will know how to guide God's people.

He will be strong and true, a lover of goodness.

He will know, love and honour God.

He will not be taken in by appearances
or by rumour or gossip.

He will judge the weak fairly and sensitively.

He will protect the rights of the poor and the helpless.

He will rule with faithfulness and love.

He will restore peace and harmony
to the whole world.

The wolf will live with the lamb.

The panther will lie down with the kid.

The calf and the young lion will eat together,
and a little child will lead them.

Cows and bears will eat together,
and their calves and cubs will sleep together.

Lions will eat straw like cattle.

No one will come to any harm.

A young child will play by the den of a poisonous snake,
a baby will put its hand into that lair;
no harm or hurt will come to them.

The land will be filled with the knowledge
of God as the seas are filled with water.

Prophets

Let the whole world be glad!

(based on Isaiah 35:1-6, 9,10)

Let the desert and the dry lands be glad!

Let the wasteland exult and rejoice!

Like clusters of sweet-smelling flowers
let the wilderness burst into bloom.

Let it be happy and sing for joy!

It will be as beautiful as the mountains of Lebanon.

As green and fruitful as Carmel and Sharon.

Everyone will recognise the glory of God.

Everyone will see God's splendour and power.

Give strength to hands that are weary.

Steady knees that are trembling with weakness.

Say to all those who are faint hearted,

"Courage, be strong. Do not be afraid.
Here is your God, coming to save you."

Then the blind will be able to see,
and the deaf will be able to hear.

Those who are lame will leap and dance.

Those who are dumb will shout for joy.

Everyone will sing and shout with gladness.

Everlasting joy will be seen on their faces.

They will be happy forever,
free from all sorrow and sadness.

Prophets

Here is your God! (based on Isaiah 40:1-5, 9-11, 28-31)

Console my people, console them, says your God.

Speak to their hearts
and tell them
that their sins are forgiven.

Prepare for God's coming.

A voice cries out,
"Prepare a way for our God in the wilderness.

Make a straight path across the desert.

Let every valley be filled in.

Let every mountain and hill be levelled.

Then the glory of God will be made known,
and the whole human race will see it."

Go up to the top of a high mountain
joyful messenger to my people
shout as loud as you can.

Proclaim the good news for everyone to hear.

Say to them all, "Here is your God!"

Your God is coming: strong, powerful,
true and dependable.

Your God is coming like a shepherd,
feeding the flock, gathering the lambs
holding them close.

Yes, God is coming like a shepherd,
looking after the mother ewes,
leading them to a place where
they can rest.

God does not grow tired or weary.

God is most understanding.

God gives strength to those who are
tired, to those who are weak.

Young people can get tired and weary;
they can stumble and fall over,
but those who hope in God will get
their strength back.

They will feel as though they can fly
as high as eagles, run and never grow
weary, walk and never get tired.

Prophets

God's People (based on Isaiah 58:3-8)

God says: Be clear about what is right and what pleases me!

Giving up things and putting on a miserable face does not impress me.

What brings me joy is everything that brings freedom:
a kindly word for someone who is worried;
a helping hand for someone in trouble.

When people share food with the hungry
and help the homeless find shelter;
if they give clothes to those in need
and work at bringing happiness to their family and friends,

I see my love growing in them.

This is what pleases me,
and they will become signs of hope for everyone,
like a bright sunrise after a long, dark night.

Prophets

HERE I AM! (based on Isaiah 58:9-11)

Cry, and God will answer.

Call, and God will say, 'Here I am'.

If you do away with the clenched fist and malicious words,
if you deprive yourself for the hungry
and give to those in need,
then your light will rise in the darkness
and sadness will be turned into joy.

God will always guide you.

God will always give you what you need.

God will give you strength.

You will be like a well-watered garden,
like a spring of water that never runs dry.

'a well-watered garden, a spring of water that never runs dry.'

For people in climates where rainfall is seasonal, water is very important. In the lands of the Middle East, water is precious, and gardens and fountains are enjoyed and valued in a special way. Images of gardens, springs, rain and fountains are found in many places in Scripture.

Prophets

GOOD NEWS FOR THE POOR (based on Isaiah 61:1-2,10-11)

The spirit of God has been given to me.

God has sent me to bring good news to the poor,
to comfort the broken hearted,
to set free those who are imprisoned
to proclaim that the time has come
when God will shower blessings on his people.

My heart is filled with joy,
with praise and thanks to God.

I feel as if God has surrounded me with love,
as if God has wrapped me up in a cloak of blessings.

I feel like a bride dressed for her wedding, adorned in jewels.

For just as surely as the earth sends up green shoots, just as surely as the garden makes seeds grow, so will God bring love and justice and praise to people.

GOD IS COMING! (based on Isaiah 62:11-12)

This is what God proclaims
to the ends of the earth.

Look, your Saviour comes
bringing with him all that
he has done for you.

You will be called:

God's Holy People;
The People God has saved;
The City that God loves;
The City that God did not forget or abandon;
The City to which God is always faithful.

Christ the Redeemer high above the city of Rio de Janeiro

God's Holy People or 'People of God'.

This name reminded the Jewish people that God chose them. The early Christians and the Church today use the same name. It is a reminder that the Church is the People God calls to be one family.

Prophets

God says (based on Jeremiah 33:14-15)

God told me: "The time is coming,
when I will make good the promise of happiness
I made to the people of Israel.

Then I will choose a king from the family of King David.

That king will do what is right and just for everyone."

What do you like best in these readings?

Who are the people in need who might like to hear these promises?

I will forgive you (based on Ezekiel 36:24-28)

I am going to gather you together and bring you home.

I will pour clean water over you, and you will be clean again.

I will forgive you your sins.

I will make you new again, and you will be full of love.

I will take away your hard heart and give you a kind heart in its place.

I will put my spirit in you, and you will do what is right.

You will be my people, and I will be your God.

Change!

(based on Joel 2:12-13)

Change! Come back to me with all your heart.

Make a new start.

Turn to me for I am kind and understanding,

loving and gentle.

I am always ready to forgive you.

I will never change.

Prophets

My love for you is great (based on Hosea 11:1-4)

I have always loved you, my people.

My love for you is so great.

I have walked every step with you on your journey.

I have always tried to keep you close to me,
but so often you have wandered away.

I gathered you up in my arms,
but you did not recognise that I was taking care of you.

I picked you up and held you close to my cheek.

I held you so close, with such great love.

Make sure justice is for all

(based on Amos 5:14-15)

Always aim to do what is good
and avoid what is evil,
so that you will live as God's people;
and when you say that your God is with you,
it really will be true.

Hate what is wrong; love what is right.

Make sure that justice is done for everyone
so that your God will show mercy to you.

God sings for joy!

(based on Zephaniah 3:14-15, 17-19)

Sing and shout for joy.

Rejoice with all your heart.

The Lord, the king of Israel, is with you;
there is no reason now to be afraid.

The Lord, your God, is with you.

The Lord will take delight
in you and in his love he
will give you new life.

He will sing and be joyful over you,
as joyful as people at a festival.

The time is coming!

Prophets

THE NEW TESTAMENT

Matthew, Mark, Luke and John are called Evangelists.

In the four gospels, they tell us how God came to us in a man whose name was Jesus.

MARK wants us to know Jesus who shares our loneliness, fear and courage. Mark's symbol is a lion.

MATTHEW reminds us that Jesus teaches us how to live with God who is always with us. Matthew's symbol is a person.

LUKE tells us how Jesus seeks people who are lost to bring them to God. Luke's symbol is a bull.

JOHN wants us to know Jesus, the One who wants us to have the fullness of life. John's symbol is an eagle.

Mark is the earliest gospel. It was written in Rome and contains a lot of Peter's preaching. Matthew and Luke revised and added to the gospel of Mark for their own local churches.

John's was the last of the four Gospels to be written, probably about sixty or seventy years after the death and resurrection of Jesus. The stories of Jesus had been told and retold many times. John's gospel is written in a different style from the other three. It is more reflective and caught up in the mystery and glory of Jesus' life, death and resurrection.

Each of the evangelists tells of the coming of Jesus in a different way.

Gospels

THE COMING OF JESUS

Each of the evangelists tells of the coming of Jesus in a different way.

Luke and Matthew tell the stories of the childhood of Jesus. (pp69-79)

Jesus' birth was Good News to the poor shepherds (Luke), to rich men (Matthew), to the Jewish people (Luke) and the Gentiles – people who were not Jews (Matthew).

The first message is: Jesus has come to all. The baby in the manger is Christ the Lord. Jesus, the promised Saviour, is worthy of homage, adoration and praise.

Mark tells of the Baptism of Jesus. (p80)

John's beginning is like a beautiful poem: Jesus is good news for the whole world. (p81)

A FAMILY TREE (based on Matthew 1:1-17)

Matthew begins with a family tree. He wants his Jewish listeners to know that Jesus is a descendant of Abraham, and of David, the great king.

Jesus came from a long line of ancestors that we can trace right back to Abraham.

From Abraham to King David the list includes:

Abraham, the father of Isaac,
Isaac, the father of Jacob,
Jacob, the father of Judah and his brothers.

Boaz was the father of Obed, Ruth being his mother,
Obed was the father of Jesse,
and Jesse was the father of King David.

David was the father of Solomon.

Finally, we come to Matthan who was the father of Jacob and Jacob was the father of Joseph, the husband of Mary, the mother of Jesus who is called Christ.

FROM THE BEGINNING

The Gospel according to Luke also gives a family tree, but Luke goes all the way back to Adam, the first man. Luke is saying that Jesus is for the whole human family. (Luke 3:23-38)

Gospels

Luke is the one who tells the most stories of the birth of Jesus, and of his early life. He tells of the joy the coming of Jesus brought to Mary, to Zechariah and Elizabeth and to the shepherds who represent the poor and the outcasts.

THE ANNOUNCEMENT OF JOHN'S BIRTH

(based on Luke 1:5-23, 57-66)

Elizabeth and Zechariah had no children. They longed for a baby of their own and prayed that God would give them a child. Zechariah was a priest who prayed and worked in the Temple of Jerusalem. There were thousands of priests, so they performed their duties in turn.

Each day only one priest was chosen to offer incense. It was a great privilege, so the priests on duty used to cast lots (rather like tossing a coin) to decide who should do it and no one was allowed to do it more than once in his life. On this day, Zechariah was chosen. As he entered the sanctuary, a crowd of people prayed outside.

God sent a messenger to Zechariah. The messenger said to him, "Zechariah, do not be afraid, your prayer has been heard. Your wife Elizabeth is to bear you a son, and you must name him John. He will be your joy and delight, and many will rejoice at his birth, for he will be great in the sight of the Lord. From his very birth, he will be filled with the Holy Spirit, and he will bring back many of the people of Israel to the Lord their God, preparing for the Lord a people fit for him."

Zechariah found this so hard to believe; he was struck dumb.

When his time of service in the Temple ended, Zechariah went home. Soon his wife Elizabeth knew she was going to have a baby. "God has blessed me!" she said.

Gospels

THE ANNUNCIATION TO MARY

(based on Luke 1:26-31, 38)

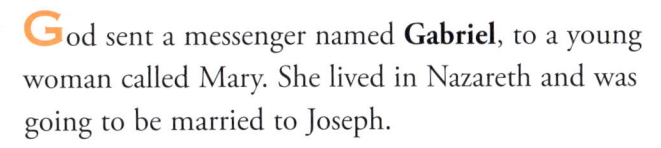

God sent a messenger named **Gabriel**, to a young woman called Mary. She lived in Nazareth and was going to be married to Joseph.

The messenger said: "Rejoice, Mary, God has blessed you and God is very close to you."

Mary did not understand these words. She was worried and wondered what it all meant.

Then Gabriel said: "Don't be afraid, Mary.

You have pleased God very much. Listen! You are going to have a baby. It will be a boy, and his name will be Jesus. He will be great and will be called the Son of God."

Then Mary said: "I want to please God. I am happy to do whatever God wants."

And the messenger left her.

Annunciation

God's message is made known to Mary. Remember 'to announce'. The church celebrates this on the 25th March. The Annunciation is the first Joyful Mystery of the Rosary.

Gabriel

God's messenger: Gabriel means 'God is strong'. The messengers of God are often pictured as angels. An angel is always a sign of a special message from God. Angels are spirits. A spirit does not have a human body, but artists paint angels with wings to remind us that the angels are ready to do what God wants without delay. The Bible pictures heaven like a royal court where angels praise God.

Gospels

The Visitation (based on Luke 1:39-58)

Mary heard that her cousin Elizabeth was also going to have a baby. Elizabeth lived in the hill country of Judah. Mary went as quickly as she could to visit her. She went into Elizabeth's house and called out to her. As soon as Elizabeth heard Mary calling, her heart was filled with joy, and she said, "I am filled with happiness because you have come to visit me. Even my baby jumped when I heard your voice. God has blessed you, and God is very close to you. Your baby will be a very special child."

And Mary said,

"God is so good. My heart is full of joy.

God has blessed me very specially.

God has done great things for me.

Holy is God's name.

God's love lasts forever.

God always helps those who ask.

God is always very close."

Mary stayed with Elizabeth for three months and then went home.

Elizabeth had a little boy. When her family and friends heard about the new baby, they shared her joy.

Gospels

The Birth of John (based on Luke 1:57-79)

The time came for Elizabeth to have her baby and she gave birth to a son. Her neighbours and relatives heard how God had blessed her, and they all rejoiced with her.

When the baby was a week old, they were going to give him the name Zechariah, after his father, but his mother said, "No! His name is John."

They said to her, "But you have no relatives with that name!"

Then they made signs to his father, asking him what name he would like the boy to have. Zechariah asked for a writing tablet and wrote, "His name is John."

At that moment Zechariah was able to speak again. He began to praise and thank God.

Zechariah was filled with the Holy Spirit and prayed:

Let us praise the God of Israel
for God has visited us and set us free.

God has given us a saviour,
who comes from the family of David,
as promised to the prophets long ago.

God promised to save us from our enemies,
from all those who hate us;
to love our ancestors;
to remember the promise to them.

God promised our father, Abraham,
that we would be free from fear,
safe from our enemies,
so that we could serve God
and live in love and goodness all our days.

You, my little child,
you will be called Prophet of the Most High,
for you will go before the Lord
to prepare a way for Him.

You will tell people to turn away from sin.
You will tell them of God's everlasting love,
You will tell them of the One who is to come
to bring light to those in darkness
to show people the way of peace.

Mary's response to Elizabeth is known as the Magnificat. It is used as part of the evening prayers of the Church all over the world each day.

Zechariah's prayer is known as the Benedictus. It is used as part of the morning prayers of the Church all over the world each day.

Gospels

THE BIRTH OF JESUS

(based on Luke 2:1-7)

Caesar Augustus, the Roman emperor, gave the order for a census to be taken over the whole Roman Empire. This was the first time that this had been done. Everyone had to go to his or her family town to be registered. So Joseph set out from Nazareth in Galilee and travelled to Judea' to Bethlehem, the town of David because he was of the family of David, and Mary went with him. She was expecting her baby and while they were there, the time came for her baby to be born. She wrapped him in swaddling clothes and put him in a manger because there was no room for them in the house.

swaddling clothes

In Jesus' time, when babies were born they were wrapped tightly in a linen cloth so that only their faces could be seen. This cloth was about thirty centimetres wide. The baby's arms were placed straight by its sides and bound close to its body. Its legs were pulled straight and tied tightly together. People thought that if they did this, the baby's bones would grow straight and strong. Today, new mothers are shown how to swaddle babies to make them feel warm and comforted as if they are snug in someone's arms. Instead of a cloth, they use a shawl.

manger

A wooden or stone trough in which the cattle feed was placed. Mary used it as a safe place for her baby.

Gospels

THE SHEPHERDS   (based on Luke 2:8-20)

That night when Jesus was born, there were some shepherds in a field nearby looking after their sheep. Suddenly the sky became light, and a messenger from God appeared. The shepherds were terrified, but the messenger of God said, "Don't be afraid, God has sent me to bring you news of great joy. This is a special night for everyone on earth. Tonight a baby called Jesus has been born in Bethlehem. He is Christ the Lord. You will find him warmly wrapped up and lying in a manger."

When the messenger had finished speaking, the shepherds could hear the sound of many voices praising God.

"Glory to God in the highest and peace to God's people on earth."

The shepherds were very excited and said to one another, "Let us go to Bethlehem to see all this."

So they hurried away and found Mary and Joseph, and the baby lying in the manger.

They told everyone what had happened and everyone was amazed.

Mary listened to their story and remembered it and thought about it often.

The shepherds went back praising and thanking God for all they had seen and heard.

Except for Mary and Joseph, the first to be told the news of the birth of Jesus were the shepherds on the hillside outside Bethlehem. They were poor men and not at all important, yet they were chosen to be the first to know about the Son whom God had sent into the world to tell everyone of God's love for us.

Gospels

Matthew tells of other visitors, the wise men who came from the East. In this way, he reminds us that the news of the birth of Jesus is for the whole world. The wise men were not Jews.

THE BIRTH OF JESUS: WISE MEN

(based on Matthew 2:1-12, 16-18)

Jesus was born in the town of Bethlehem in Judea while Herod was king. Some wise men came from the East to Jerusalem. They asked: "Where is the baby who will be king of the Jews? We have seen his star rise and have come to worship him."

When Herod, the king, heard this he was very worried and so was everyone else in Jerusalem. He called together all the chief priests and scribes of the people. He asked them where the Christ was to be born. They told him, "In the town of Bethlehem in Judea."

This is what the prophet wrote a long time ago.

"And you Bethlehem, in the land of Judah, you are important. For from you shall come a leader who will guide my people Israel."

Herod called the wise men to a secret meeting. He found out from them the exact date the star had appeared and then sent them on to Bethlehem, saying, "Go and make a careful search for the child. When you have found him let me know so that I too may go and worship him."

So they went on their way. Suddenly the star, which they had seen rising, went before them until it came to rest over the place where the child was. When they saw the star, they were delighted. They went into the house, and they saw the child with Mary, his mother. They knelt down and worshipped him. They opened their treasures and offered him gifts of gold and frankincense and myrrh. God warned them in a dream not to go back to Herod. So they returned to their own country by a different way.

Herod was furious when he saw he had been tricked by the wise men. He gave orders to kill all the male children who were two years old or under in Bethlehem and in all that region.

Gospels

Epiphany procession in Ethiopia.

Matthew doesn't tell us how many wise men there were, but everyone supposes there were three because of the three gifts. The feast of the wise men is on January 6th and is known as the Epiphany. This means 'showing' and recalls how Jesus is shown to the Gentiles. Gold is a gift for a king and recalls that Jesus is king of all creation. Frankincense is pure incense, which is burned to symbolise prayer rising to God, and is a sign that Jesus is God. Myrrh was used to anoint the bodies of the dead, and so is a sign that Jesus, because he was a man, would suffer and die.

JOSEPH'S DREAM (based on Matthew 2:13-15, 19-23)

The wise men went back to their own country. They took a different road from the one by which they had come. They knew Herod was jealous and afraid and would harm the child if he found out where he was.

After they had gone a messenger from God spoke to Joseph in a dream, "Get up, take the child and his mother with you. Herod will be searching for him, in order to kill him. Escape to Egypt and stay there until I tell you it is safe to leave."

So Joseph got up and took the child and his mother with him. They left during the night for Egypt where they stayed until Herod died.

Some time later when Joseph heard that Herod was dead, he took the child and his mother back to Israel. He was afraid to go back to Bethlehem in case Herod's son, Archelaus would harm the child, so he went to Galilee and made his home in a town called Nazareth.

Gospels

The Presentation (based on Luke 2:23-39)

The Law says that the eldest boy in each family must be taken to the temple to be presented to God. The family must also offer a pair of doves or two pigeons.

When Mary and Joseph brought Jesus to the temple, they met an old man called Simeon. Simeon was a good and holy person. He often went to the temple to pray.

Simeon took Jesus in his arms and blessed God saying: "Now I am very happy to die because you have kept your promise. I am holding the one who is to be a light for everyone in the world."

Mary and Joseph were very surprised by Simeon's words and did not quite understand what he meant.

After that, they met Anna who was an old lady. She was 84 years old. She spent all her time in the temple praying to God. She thanked God when she saw Jesus and told everyone that he would bring happiness to those who loved God.

When they had done all they had to do, Mary and Joseph took Jesus home to Nazareth where he grew up in God's love.

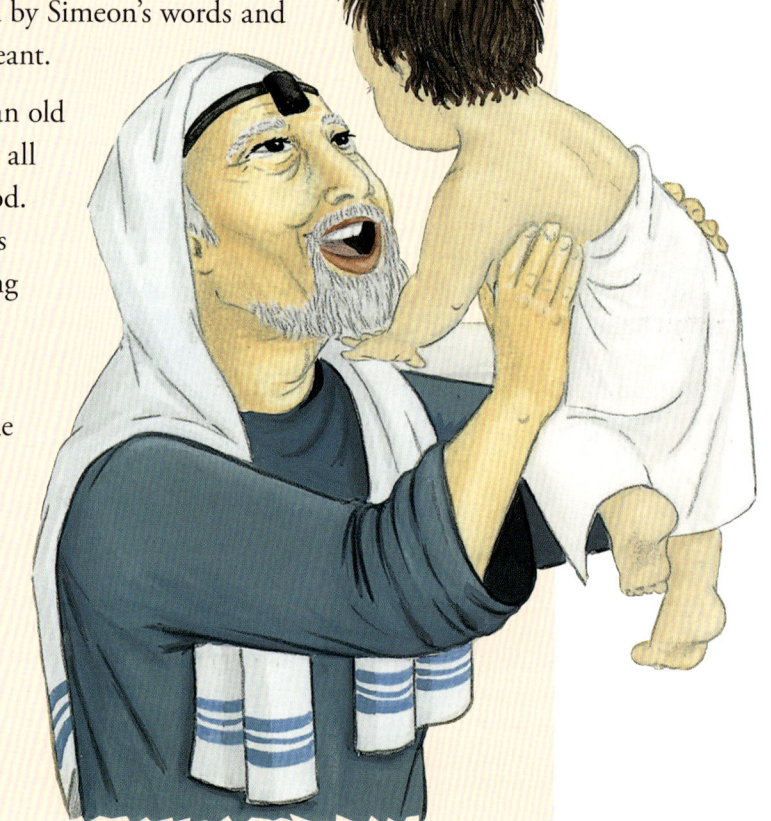

Gospels

My Father's House (based on Luke 2:40-51)

Every year Mary and Joseph went to the Temple in Jerusalem to celebrate the feast of the Passover. When Jesus was twelve years old, he went with them.

When the feast was over, Mary and Joseph set off for home without Jesus, although they didn't know it. When they realised he was not with them or with his friends, they turned back to Jerusalem to look for him.

After three days they found him in the Temple sitting among the teachers, listening to them and asking questions. Everyone was surprised at how wise he was.

Mary and Joseph were overcome when they saw him.

Mary said to him, "We have been so worried and looking for you."

"Why were you worried?" asked Jesus. "You should have known that I would be in my Father's house."

Mary and Joseph didn't understand what he meant.

He went back home to Nazareth with them and lived there obedient to his parents and growing in love and wisdom.

The Joyful Mysteries

The Annunciation
The Visitation
The Nativity (Birth of Jesus)
The Presentation in the Temple
The Finding in the Temple

These events of the childhood of Jesus make up the Joyful Mysteries of the Rosary. The Rosary is a prayer. People ask Mary, the mother of Jesus, to help them to remember the life of Jesus and come to know him better.

Gospels

The Gospel according to Mark begins with John the Baptist announcing the coming of Jesus. People went to see and hear him and John baptised them in the river Jordan.

YOU ARE MY SON **(based on Mark 1:9-11)**

Not long afterwards Jesus came from Nazareth in Galilee and was baptised by John in the River Jordan. As he was coming up out of the water the Spirit came down upon him, and a voice from heaven said, "You are my son, whom I love."

Gospels

The Gospel according to John begins quite differently. He, too, tells of the beginning of Jesus' life in this world, but he does it in a different, deeper way. The beginning of his gospel is like a beautiful poem, which describes the coming of Jesus as good news for the whole world. He writes of Jesus 'the Word' of God.

IN THE BEGINNING (based on John 1:1-4 8, 13-14, 16-18)

In the beginning was the Word, God's Word.

Through the Word, all things came to be.

All that came to be was alive with God's life,
not one thing came into being except through God's Word.

The Word was the real light,
the light that was coming into the world,
the light that would give light to everyone.

The Word became a man
he lived among us full of grace and truth.

We saw his glory, the glory which he received
from the Father as the Father's Only Son.

From the fullness of his glory
he has blessed us all with gift after gift.

No one has ever seen God,
it is the Only Son who is nearest to the Father's heart
who has made him known.

John tells us that everyone and everything in creation came into being by the power of God's Word.

Words are very powerful. They can be the way to something wonderful like a new friendship or a new way of living. They can make a real difference to people's lives.

Gospels

THE GOSPEL ACCORDING TO MATTHEW

Jesus, the Teacher

Matthew's gospel collects Jesus' teaching in what is called the Sermon on the Mount. (Chs 5-7) Matthew's Jewish readers would remember Mount Sinai and how Moses brought God's law to the People. In Matthew's gospel Jesus says very clearly, "I have not come to do away with the Law or the teachings of the prophets." Matthew wants his readers to recognise Jesus as the 'new Moses' calling all people to a new way of living.

A NEW WAY OF LIVING (based on Matthew 5: 1-17)

When he saw the crowds, Jesus went up the mountain and sat down. His disciples gathered round him, and this is what he taught them.

You will be blessed when you have an open and generous heart.
When you share what you have with other people, God will be very close to you.

You will be blessed when you reach out to those who grieve.
When you make friends with those who are sad and lonely, God will be there to comfort you.

You will be blessed when you are gentle.
When you treat others with kindness
and patience, God will give you all you need.

You will be blessed when you work for justice.
When you respect and stand up for the rights of others, God will give you life to the full.

You will be blessed when you forgive others and don't hold grudges.
You will find God ready to forgive you.

You will be blessed when you desire what is good.
When you always search for what is good, you will find God in all around you.

You will be blessed when you are a peacemaker.
When you try not to let a quarrel even begin or are first to say sorry, you will be known as children of God.

You will be blessed when you are made fun of for doing what God wants.
When people laugh at you for living in God's way, know that you are very close to God.

Remember what happened to so many of God's messengers.

Rejoice and be glad.

Gospels 83

Go Further

"The Law says, 'You shall not kill.'

But I say this to you.

Don't hold anger against your brother or sister.

Anyone who calls a brother or sister names or looks down on him or her as 'good-for-nothing' will be in danger of going to the fire of hell

(based on Matthew 5:17, 20, 23-24)

The Law says, 'An eye for an eye, and a tooth for a tooth'.

But I say this to you.

Do not try to get your own back when someone hurts you.

Always be generous and forgiving.

Never set out to get revenge.

If someone asks you for something, give it and more.

If someone wants to borrow something, lend it willingly.

(based on Matthew 5:17, 20, 23-24)

You have learned 'You must love your neighbour and hate your enemy'.

But I say this to you:

Love your enemies and pray for those who persecute you;
in this way, you will be sons and daughters of God.

God's love is like the sun, which rises each day and gives warmth and light to everyone, not just good people.

God sends rain to water the earth and the rain falls on the honest and the dishonest people alike.

Don't just love people who love you!

Don't just talk to the people who are your friends!

No, I tell you, your love must be like God's love.

God loves everyone no matter who they are or what they do.

You must not put any limits on your love, for the love of your Father in heaven is never-ending, never-changing.

(based on Matthew 5:44-48)

Hell

Hell is the name we give to separation from God, and from the joy of knowing God's love. God invites each person to share this love but leaves each one free to accept or reject the invitation to love God and to love others for God's sake. Artists and writers picture hell as a place of fire, smoke and darkness. These are metaphors for the loss of love and life with God.

About Giving (based on Matthew 6:2-4)

When you give something to someone in need, don't go around boasting about what you have done. This is what people who want to show off do. They are not really generous. They do it so that people will see them and tell them how wonderful they are. I tell you, they already have had their reward.

When you help someone in need, don't tell anyone. Do it so that even your best friends know nothing about it, and your Father in heaven who knows what is in your heart will reward you.

About Real Treasure

(based on Matthew 6:19-21)

Do not store up riches for yourselves here on earth.

Moths and woodworms may eat them, rust may ruin them, or thieves can break in and steal them.

No, store up real treasures for yourself in heaven.

Moths and woodworm, rust and thieves cannot touch these.

Set your heart on what is really important.

For wherever your treasure is, that is where your heart will be.

About Knowing Yourself

(based on Matthew 7:1-5)

Don't judge other people, for God will judge you in the same way as you judge others. When you apply rules to others, remember, God will apply rules to you in the same way. Why do you see the least thing wrong that someone else does and don't notice the worse thing wrong that you are doing? It's like seeing a speck of dust in someone else's eye and not noticing a huge wooden beam in your own! First take the wooden beam out of your own eye and you will see more clearly to take the speck out of someone else's eye.

Gospels

ABOUT TRUSTING GOD (based on Matthew 6:24-31)

No one can serve two different people well. When you give time to one, you don't have much time left for the other. When you give your loyalty totally to one, you end up being less loyal to the other.

You cannot serve both God and money.

This is why I tell you don't worry about your life,

and what to eat and drink and what to wear.

Life is about more than all these things,

and your body is worth more than your clothes!

Look at the birds! They don't sow seeds, or gather the crops at harvest time and store them in barns, yet your Father in heaven takes care of them.

Surely you are worth much more than birds?

Can you, however hard you try, or however much you worry about it, add even one more day to your life?

And why worry about clothes?

Look at the wild flowers. They do not work or make clothes for themselves, but I tell you that not even King Solomon in his royal robes was dressed as beautifully as one of these.

If God takes such care over wild flowers that are here today and will be gone by tomorrow, won't he take even greater care of you?

Believe in God's love for you. Do not worry! Don't say, 'what will I eat? What will I drink? What will I wear?' Your Father in heaven knows that you need all these things.

Instead, set your hearts on the Kingdom of God and what God wants for you, and God will take care of all your needs.

Gospels

ABOUT PRAYER (based on Matthew 7:7-11)

Ask, and you will be given what you ask.

Search, and you will find what you are looking for.

Knock, and the door will be opened for you.

Do you know any parents who love their children and won't feed them when they are hungry?

If mothers and fathers know how to give their children what is good for them, how much more will your Father in heaven give good things to those who ask for them.

How would the people who heard Jesus have felt?

What is your favourite sentence?

How does it make you feel?

REMEMBER!

(based on Matthew 7:12)

Treat other people as you would like them to treat you.

Do to them what you would like them to do to you.

Care for them in all the ways you would like them to care for you.

This is what the Law and the teachings of the prophets really mean.

Gospels

A Parable from Matthew's Gospel (based on Matthew 25:31-40)

One day Jesus was talking to his friends. He was telling them a **parable** about how God will judge everyone at the end of time. The story pictures a king sitting on his royal throne with people from all nations gathered around him. He will divide them into two groups, one on his right, the other on his left.

Then he will say to the people on his right,

"Come, you are blessed by my Father.
Come and live in the kingdom,
which has been prepared for you since
the beginning of the world.

When I was hungry, you gave me food to eat.

When I was thirsty, you gave me something to drink.

When I was a stranger, you took me into your home.

When I was without clothes, you shared yours with me.

When I was ill, you took care of me.

When I was in prison, you came to visit me."

They will say to the king,

"When did we see you hungry and give you food to eat?

When did we see you thirsty and give you something to drink?

When did we see you a stranger and take you home with us?

When did we see you without clothes and share ours with you?

When did we see you ill and take care of you?

When did we see you in prison and come to visit you?"

And the King will reply,

"Whenever you did these things for any one of my brothers and sisters you did them for me."

> *Parable*
>
> *When we try to explain things to other people, it is often easier to tell them a story. Jesus told stories called parables. A parable does not work out the way people expect. A parable can have more than one meaning, and the ending is often surprising.*
>
> What does this parable tell you about Jesus?
>
> What do you think the king will say to the group of people on his left?

Gospels

THE GOSPEL ACCORDING TO MARK

Jesus, the Son of God

Mark begins his gospel 'This is the good news about Jesus Christ, the Son of God'. All that Jesus says and does is good news of God his Father and God's love. The apostles Jesus calls to be with him, the sick, the poor and people in trouble all find that Jesus is a friend whose love is the greatest. Mark's Gospel shows how Jesus' apostles found it hard to understand that his death was to be the sign of how much God loves everyone. They discovered that choosing to be a friend of Jesus means tough choices.

GOOD NEWS OF GOD (based on Mark 1:14-20)

Jesus went into Galilee. He proclaimed the **Good News** of God saying, "The right time has come. The **Kingdom of God** is very near. Turn away from your sins and believe the Good News of God's love."

As he was walking along the shore of Lake Galilee, he saw Simon and his brother Andrew. They were fishermen, and they were casting a net to catch fish.

Jesus said to them, "Come, follow me. I will make you fishers of people." At once they left their nets and went after him.

A little further on Jesus saw James and John, the sons of Zebedee. They were in their boat mending their nets. Jesus called to them, "Come, follow me." They left their father Zebedee in the boat and went with Jesus.

Good News
The message of God's love and forgiveness that Jesus came to tell everyone. 'Gospel' means 'good news'.

Kingdom of God
Not a place. When everyone is faithful to God's way of love and peace and keeps God's commandments: that is the Kingdom of God. It is another way of speaking about the new life God has prepared for everyone.

I HAVE CHOSEN YOU (based on Mark 3:13-19)

Jesus left the crowds behind and went up onto the mountain. He sent for some of his friends. When they came, he chose twelve of them to be his special friends and to help him in his work. "I have chosen you to be my apostles," he said, "I want to send you out to tell everyone the Good News of God's love."

These are the names of the twelve:

Simon (whom Jesus called Peter – the rock);
James and John, the sons of Zebedee (whom Jesus called sons of thunder);
Andrew; Philip; Bartholomew; Matthew; Thomas;
James the son of Alphaeus; Thaddaeus; Simon the Zealot
and Judas Iscariot (he would, one day, betray Jesus).

WHO IS THE GREATEST? (based on Mark 9:33-35)

Jesus and his friends made their way through Galilee until they came to Capernaum. Jesus had heard some of them arguing on the way.

When he got into the house where they were staying, he asked them, "What were you arguing about on the road?" They didn't answer him because they had been arguing about which of them was the greatest.

So Jesus sat down with the twelve and said to them, "The greatest will be the one who is kindest, who shows the most love and care. The greatest is the one who puts others first."

Tradition says these ruins of a first-century church are on the place where Peter lived in Capernaum.

Gospels

An Invitation (based on Mark 10:17-22)

Jesus was setting out on a journey one day, when a man ran up to him, knelt on the ground before him, and asked him this question. "Good Master what must I do so that I can live forever with God?"

Jesus answered, "Only God is good. You know what you have to do because you know the **commandments**. Don't kill anyone. Don't take someone else's wife for your partner. Don't steal. Don't tell lies about people. Don't cheat people. Respect your parents."

The young man said, "Master, I've kept those commandments since I was very young."

Jesus looked straight at him and was filled with love for him. Then Jesus said, "You need to do one thing more. Go and sell everything you have and give the money to the poor. You will then be rich in God's eyes. Then come and follow me."

The young man's face changed when he heard these words, and he went away sad because he was a very wealthy man.

Commandments

Rules for living in friendship with God and with others. The Jewish people received the commandments as God's gift, given to them through Moses at Mount Sinai.

WHAT DOES GOD WANT? (based on Mark 12:28-31)

The chief priests and scribes heard about the work and teaching of Jesus. They tried to find some way of getting rid of him, but they were afraid because the people followed him. So they sent some **Pharisees** and **scribes** to ask him questions and try to catch him out. One of the scribes asked him, "What commandment is the most important of all?"

Jesus replied, "The most important one is this, 'Listen, Israel! The Lord, our God, is the only Lord. Love the Lord your God with all your heart, with all your soul, with all your mind, and with all your strength'. The second most important commandment is this: 'Love your neighbour as you love yourself'. There is no other commandment more important than these two."

IF YOU WANT TO BE MY FRIEND

Mark's gospel tells us that three times Jesus told his friends about how he must suffer and die. They found it very had to understand.

Jesus began to speak to his disciples about his suffering and death. He told them that the Son of Man was to suffer greatly and be rejected by the elders, the chief priests and the scribes and that he was to be put to death. Peter took him aside and began to protest. But Jesus turned around, looked at his disciples and said to Peter, "You are thinking in the way people do, not in the way God does."

(based on Mark 8: 31-33)

Jesus made his way through Galilee with his disciples. He did not want anyone to know where he was because he wanted to speak to them for a second time about his death. He told them, "The Son of Man will be handed over to those who will kill him." But they did not understand what he said and were too frightened to ask him.

(based on Mark 9: 30-32)

Jesus and his disciples set off for Jerusalem. The disciples were afraid, and so were the other people with them. For a third time, Jesus took the Twelve aside and spoke of the things that were going to happen to him. "We are now going up to Jerusalem, and the Son of Man is about to be handed over to the chief priests and the scribes. They will condemn him to death and hand him over to those who will make fun of him, spit upon him, whip him and put him to death."

(based on Mark 10: 32-34)

Gospels

I HAVE COME TO GIVE MY LIFE (based on Mark 10:35-45)

James and John came to Jesus and said, "Master, we want you to do something for us."

"What is it?" asked Jesus.

They said, "When you are king we want to sit on your right and your left."

Jesus answered, "You don't understand what you are asking? Can you share the sufferings I have told you I must go through?"

"We can," they replied.

Jesus said, "Yes, you shall share my suffering, but the places of honour on my right and left are not mine to decide. Only my Father knows who will be given those places."

The other disciples were angry with James and John when they heard about this. Jesus called them all together and said to them, "You have seen how rulers and leaders want power and control over people. You are to be different. Whoever wants to be great has to be at the service of everyone. I have not come to lord it over others. I have come to serve and to give my life for everyone."

What did Jesus' friends find hard to understand?

Why do you think this was hard for them?

What would you find easy?

What would you find hard?

Pharisees

Pharisees were really strict about keeping the Jewish law. They kept themselves apart from people like tax collectors, and anyone who was not Jewish.

Scribes

They were teachers of the law and spent their time studying it and discussing the details of it.

Gospels

THE GOSPEL ACCORDING TO LUKE

Jesus the Bringer of Hope and Freedom

Luke's gospel tells of Jesus, the One who brings hope and freedom for everyone. Luke shows us that some people were surprised to find themselves included. Some people were shocked to see Jesus welcome people who, at that time, were looked down on and treated as outcasts. Luke also shows us that people have to choose freedom.

WHEN THE TIME HAD COME   (based on Luke 3:23)

Luke tells us that Jesus was about thirty years old when he left Nazareth. Jesus knew the time had come for him to begin the work his Father had given him to do: to tell people about the Good News of God's great love for them.

JESUS CHOOSES GOD'S WAY   (based on Luke 4:1-13)

Jesus went out into the desert. There was nobody there; nothing but sand and rock. He was all alone for forty days. He ate nothing, so at the end of forty days, he was extremely hungry. He heard a voice telling him that he could change stones into bread if he wanted.

Jesus knew that eating was not the most important thing in life. He remembered God's word: 'No one lives on bread alone'.

Again he was **tempted**. The voice promised him all the kingdoms of the world. Jesus knew that the only true ruler of the world is God. He remembered God's word: 'I am the Lord your God, you shall serve no one before me'.

A third time the tempting voice came to Jesus. "If you are God's Son, you can do anything, and God will take care of you. Even if you threw yourself off the highest place, God would protect you." Jesus remembered God's word, 'You must not put God to the test'. The voice of the tempter was silent.

Gospels

JESUS BEGINS HIS MISSION

(based on Luke 4:14-22)

Jesus, filled with the Holy Spirit, returned to Galilee. News about him spread all through that place. He taught in the **synagogues,** and everyone praised him.

He came to Nazareth where he had been brought up and went into the synagogue as he usually did. He stood up to read. He was given the scroll of the prophet Isaiah. He unrolled the scroll and found the place and read:

"The Spirit of the Lord is upon me for he has chosen and anointed me to bring good news to the poor, to heal the broken-hearted. He has sent me to set free all those who are imprisoned or oppressed in any way."

He rolled up the **scroll**, gave it back to the synagogue attendant and sat down. All the people in the synagogue were looking at him as he said to them, "This passage of Scripture came true today while you heard it being read."

Everyone was impressed by him and marvelled at the wonderful and powerful words that he spoke.

Nazareth today.

Tempted
When we feel we want to do something, which we know or feel, is bad. When something happens, that forces us to choose between what we know is right and something we know or feel is wrong. In the Bible, the Tempter is called Satan or the devil.

Synagogue
The synagogue was the meeting-house for the local Jewish community. They gathered there on the Sabbath to pray and listen to the Word of God. It was also a school where Jewish boys learned the Scriptures.

Scroll
The Jewish Scriptures were written by hand on scrolls. These scrolls were treated with great respect and care and kept in a special place in the synagogue. This box or cupboard was called the Ark to remind the people of the special ark in which the Israelites kept the tablets of the Law on their journey through the desert.

Gospels

Those who came to hear Jesus also saw some of the wonderful ways in which he changed people's lives. Jesus also healed people and cared for their needs by working miracles. Matthew, Mark and Luke describe the miracles as powerful acts of God. John calls them signs because they point to the presence of God in Jesus. In all the gospels, the miracle stories tell us who Jesus is and why he has come. They show that, in Jesus, the power and love of God his Father, touches our world. A miracle is good news of God's love and care for people and God's presence.

JESUS CALLS LEVI (based on Luke 5:27-32)

One day Jesus noticed a tax collector called Levi sitting in the tax office. Jesus said to him, "Follow me."

Levi got up, left everything, and followed Jesus.

Levi gave a party in honour of Jesus. Among the people he invited were a large number of tax collectors and sinners. Some Pharisees and Scribes complained to the disciples, "Why does your master eat and drink with tax collectors and sinners?"

Jesus answered them, "Healthy people don't need a doctor, only sick people do."

Bread is a basic food. Do you remember the manna that the People of God ate in the desert? Luke's Jewish readers would probably remember this when they heard of Jesus feeding the people in a lonely place. In John's gospel, Jesus says, 'I am the bread of life'. Christians read of this miracle and remember that in Holy Communion Jesus gives himself.

JESUS FEEDS THE PEOPLE (based on Luke 9:12-15)

Jesus had been speaking to the crowds all day. As evening drew near his disciples came to him and said, "Send the people away so that they can go to the nearest villages to find food and shelter for the night, because this is a lonely place."

Jesus said to them, "You give them something to eat."

They answered, "We have only five loaves and two fishes. Are we to go and buy food for all these people?"

There were about five hundred men there. (Luke does not say how many women and children were also there.)

Gospels

Jesus told the twelve, "Have the people sit down in groups of about fifty." So off they went and did as he asked.

Jesus took the five loaves and the two fish. He looked up to heaven, said the blessing, broke the bread and fish and gave them to the disciples to hand out to the crowd. Everyone ate as much as they wanted. The leftovers were gathered up and filled twelve baskets.

Gospels

JESUS GIVES SIGHT TO A BLIND MAN (based on Luke 18:35-43)

One day, as Jesus was on the way to Jericho, a **blind man** was begging at the roadside. When he heard a crowd going past, he asked people what was happening. They said, "Jesus of Nazareth is passing by."

Then he began to shout loudly, "Jesus, Son of David, have mercy on me!"

The people standing at the front of the crowds got annoyed and told him to be quiet; but he shouted louder still, "Son of David, have mercy on me!"

Jesus stopped and called for him to be brought to him. He asked, "What do you want me to do for you?"

The man answered, "Lord, let me see again."

Jesus said, "Receive your sight; your faith has saved you."

At once he was able to see again and followed Jesus along the road, praising God. The people who had seen what had happened also praised God.

JESUS FORGIVES A SINNER (based on Luke 7:36, 40, 44-50)

One of the Pharisees called Simon invited Jesus to a meal. Jesus went to his house and sat down. A woman who had lived a sinful life heard that Jesus was eating at Simon's house. During the meal, she brought in an alabaster jar of sweet-smelling ointment and began washing Jesus' feet.

Simon didn't think much of her because everyone said she was a **sinner**.

Jesus said to Simon, "You see this woman, she has washed my feet with her tears, wiped them with her hair, anointed them with her ointment. You, Simon, did not wash or dry my feet. Nor did you anoint my head with oil."

Jesus said, "Everything she has done wrong is forgiven her. She has shown great love." He told the woman, "Your sins are forgiven."

Everyone at the meal began to say, "Who can this man be if he forgives sins?"

Gospels

THE WOMEN (based on Luke 8:1-3)

Jesus travelled through towns and villages preaching and proclaiming the Good News. The twelve disciples went with him as well as some **women.** Among them were Mary, whose surname was Magdalene, Joanna whose husband Chuza worked at Herod's court and Susanna. There are many other women, who used their own resources, to help Jesus and his disciples.

blind man

In Mark's Gospel, you will find the same story with this difference: the blind man is named Bartimaeus.

Sinner

To the Pharisees, anyone who did not keep God's law in every detail was a sinner. Simon was shocked to see Jesus accept this service from a woman who was known to be a sinner.

'Simon, you did not wash or dry my feet; nor did you anoint my head'. These would have been polite ways to greet a guest who had travelled over dusty roads.

Women

At the time of Jesus, it would have been unusual for women to be included among the disciples of a great Teacher. Luke is reminding his readers that the Good News is for everyone and that in the Kingdom of God everyone is equal. Luke also tells us it was the women who were the first to tell the good news of the resurrection. (The empty tomb p113)

Gospels

WHO IS MY NEIGHBOUR? (based on Luke 10:25-37)

One day Jesus was asked a tricky question about God's law by a teacher of the law who wanted to catch Jesus out. He came to Jesus and asked, "What must I do so that I will live with God forever?" Jesus answered with a question, "What does it tell you, in the law?"

The teacher of the law answered, "Love the Lord your God with all your heart with all your strength and with all your mind, and love your neighbour as yourself."

Jesus said, "That's right. So go and do what the law says."

Then the teacher asked another question, "Who is my neighbour?" He was still hoping to catch Jesus out. Then Jesus told one of his stories, a parable.

There was once a man going on a journey from Jerusalem to Jericho when robbers set upon him. They stripped him of his clothes, beat him up and left him half dead. A priest happened to pass by; he saw the man lying injured and walked by on the other side of the road. Then a lawyer came along. He went over and had a look at the man; then he too walked away on the other side of the road.

Next came a **Samaritan**. When he saw the poor injured man lying in the ditch, his heart was filled with pity. He went over to him, poured oil and wine on his wounds to clean them and bandaged them up. Then he helped the man climb up on his own animal and took him to an inn, where he could rest and be looked after. Next day the Samaritan gave the innkeeper two silver coins. "Take care of him till he's better," he told the innkeeper, and when I come back this way, I'll repay you whatever else you've spent on him."

Jesus ended the story with a question, "Which of the three was a neighbour to the man?"

Samaritan

The Samaritans lived in Samaria. Jews and Samaritans would have nothing to do with one another. How do you think Jesus' audience would have felt when he used a Samaritan as an example of a good neighbour?

Gospels

Gospels 101

The Parable of the prodigal son (based on Luke 15:11-32)

A man had two sons. The younger became impatient of living at home on the farm. He wanted to set out into the wide world and seek his fortune. He said to his father, "Father, give me my share of the money from the farm that would come to me when you die."

His father was very sad to hear this, but he loved his son, so he sold off half the farm and gave him the money.

The older brother was furious, but the younger son was delighted. He had never had so much money in his life! At once he set off for a far country where nobody would know him, and his riches would impress everyone. And they were impressed! He soon found friends to help him to spend his money. He really enjoyed himself. He did anything he wanted. There would be plenty of time later to get a job and come home to his family a very wealthy man.

But a famine spread quickly over the country. Crops failed, and there was very little work of any sort to be had. His new friends could not even be bothered to offer him a meal. The only job he could find was working on the farm of a Gentile – feeding pigs! He was so hungry that he would have been glad to eat the pigs' food himself. At last, he came to his senses.

"Even my father's servants have more food than they want, and here am I dying of hunger! I will leave this place and go to my father and say: "Father, I have sinned against heaven, and against you; I don't deserve to be called your son; treat me as one of your paid servants." So he left the place and went back to his father.

His father had been watching out, hoping his son would come home. While he was still a long way off, his father saw him, barefoot, ragged and dirty and so very pale and thin. He ran to the boy and hugged and kissed him.

The son began his speech, but his father interrupted him, calling to the servants, "Quick! Bring out the best robe and put it on him; put a ring on his finger and sandals on his feet. Bring the calf we have been fattening and prepare a feast. I want to celebrate because this son of mine was dead and has come back to life; he was lost and is found."

Gospels

prodigal

'Prodigal' has two meanings – 'free and easy, wasteful' and 'generous'. The son is called 'the prodigal' because he is so free in spending his money.

Is there anyone else in the story who is 'prodigal'?

What would you have said to help the elder brother understand what his father had done?

So the celebrations began. Soon his elder brother came in from the fields hot, tired and hungry. He heard the music and dancing and wanted to know what it was all about. When the servants explained, he was angry and refused to go in, even when his father came out and tried to persuade him.

All he would say was, "I've stayed with you all my life, obeyed you and worked for you, and you never once put on a celebration for my friends. Yet, when this good-for-nothing comes home after wasting all your money, you have a feast." His father said, "My son, you are with me always, and all I have is yours. But it was only right we should celebrate and rejoice because your brother here was dead and has come to life; he was lost and is found."

Gospels

LORD, TEACH US TO PRAY (based on Luke 11:1-4)

Jesus was praying one day. When he had finished, one of the disciples said,

"Lord, will you teach us to pray?"

Jesus said to them, "When you pray, say this:

Father, let everyone honour your holy name.

May everyone live in your love and friendship.

May we all have enough to eat every day.

Forgive us when we do something wrong

because we forgive anyone who has hurt us.

And be with us if we have to make difficult choices."

> Matthew's gospel also gives a version of the prayer Jesus taught his friends. It has become the prayer of all Christian disciples. It is called 'the Lord's Prayer' or 'the Our Father'.

THE GOOD SHEPHERD (based on Luke 15:3-6,7)

One day Jesus said, "Suppose one of you has a hundred sheep and loses one of them. What do you do? You leave the other ninety-nine sheep grazing on the hillside and go looking for the one that got lost until you find it. When you find it, you are so happy that you put it on your shoulders and carry it back home. Then you call your friends and neighbours together. "I am so happy," you say, "because I have found my lost sheep. Let's celebrate!"

"It's like that with people," Jesus told them. "If ninety-nine people stay close to God that's good. But if one who has turned away from God and done something wrong says sorry and comes back to God, then that is a reason to celebrate. God is like the good shepherd, always searching for the lost sheep, looking out the person who has turned away."

THE PHARISEE AND THE TAX COLLECTOR (based on Luke 18:9-14)

Once upon a time, there were two men – one, a Pharisee, the other a **tax collector.** They went to pray in the temple one day. The Pharisee stood up by himself and prayed this prayer.

"I thank you that I am not greedy, and I am not dishonest like everyone else. I thank you that I am not like this tax collector. I fast twice a week. I give a tenth of my wages to the temple."

The tax collector could not lift up his head to pray. His words were, "God, be merciful to me, a sinner."

Jesus said, "The tax collector, not the Pharisee, went home at peace with God."

> **tax collector**
> An official collector of taxes. No Jewish people liked paying taxes to the Roman conquerors. They especially hated Jewish people who worked as tax collectors. Because it was a hated job, the Romans allowed anyone who volunteered to overcharge and keep the money for himself.

Gospels

THE GOSPEL ACCORDING TO JOHN

Jesus, the Light and Life of the world

John's Gospel shows us Jesus, the Word of God, who makes God's love plain for everyone to see, and shows what it is that makes life worth living. John's gospel collects what Jesus taught his disciples about his Father and the Holy Spirit and about the way they were to live (Chapters 13-17). This becomes Jesus' final message to his friends at their last supper.

FINDING JESUS (based on John 1:29-42)

John the Baptist saw Jesus coming along, and he pointed him out to the people as the promised one who had come from God to save them. He was the one about whom he had said, 'One will come after me, but he is greater than I. Even I did not realise who he was in the beginning. When I baptised him with water, I knew he was filled with the Holy Spirit. He is the Son of God. Those he baptises will also be filled with the Spirit'.

The next day John was standing there again with two of his disciples when he saw Jesus walking by. "There is the Lamb of God!" he said.

The two disciples heard him say this and went after Jesus. Jesus turned, saw them following him, and asked," What are you looking for?"

They answered, "Where do you live, Rabbi?" ('Rabbi' means 'teacher'.)

"Come and see," he answered. It was then about four o'clock in the afternoon. So they went with him and saw where he lived, and spent the rest of that day with him.

One of them was Andrew, Simon Peter's brother. At once, he found his brother Simon and told him, "We have found the Messiah." ('Messiah' means 'Christ') Then he took Simon to Jesus.

Gospels

JESUS THE BREAD OF LIFE (based on John, 6:35,37,51,60,67-68)

Jesus sometimes said things that people found hard to understand. One day he said, "I am the bread of life. Anyone who becomes my friend will never be hungry. Anyone who trusts in me will never be thirsty. I will never send away from me anyone who wants to be my friend.

Anyone who trusts in me will find out what life really is. I am the living bread which comes from God. Anyone who has this bread for food will learn the secret of life that cannot be taken away. The bread I give is my life. I give it to be the life of the world."

Many of Jesus' disciples did not understand this. They went away.

Jesus asked the twelve he had chosen, "Will you also go away?"

Peter answered, "Who else could we go to? You are the one who has shown us what life really is, the kind of life that cannot be taken away."

The ruins of the synagogue in Capernaum. It is built over an earlier building where Jesus may have prayed and taught.

Gospels

Who is a sinner? (based on John 8:3-11)

Early in the morning, Jesus went to the Temple. People came to him, and he sat down to teach them.

The scribes and Pharisees brought along a woman who had broken the law. They made her stand there in the middle of everyone. "This woman has broken the law," they said to Jesus, "and in the law, it says that she should be stoned to death. What have you to say about this?"

They asked him the question because they were trying to trick him. They wanted him to say something that they could hold against him.

Jesus said nothing. He bent down and began writing in the dust with his finger. They asked the question again. He stood up and said to them, "Let anyone who has never broken the law, never done wrong, never sinned, throw the first stone at her." He bent down again and carried on writing in the dust.

When they thought about what Jesus had said, they went away one by one until the last one was gone.

Jesus was left alone with the woman who was still standing there in the middle. Jesus stood up again and asked, "Woman, where are they? Has no one condemned you?"

"No one sir," she answered.

"Neither will I," said Jesus. "Go, and from now on do what is right."

Gospels

WORDS OF LIFE (based on John 12:44-46, 49-50)

"Whoever believes in me believes in the Father who sent me, and whoever sees me sees the Father who sent me. I have come into the world as a light to prevent anyone who believes in me from being in the dark.

The words I have spoken are not my words, but the words of the Father who sent me.

I know that his commands mean eternal light and life."

A NEW RULE

(based on John 13:34-35)

Jesus said,

"I am giving you a new rule for living; love one another.

You must love one another in the same way as I have loved you.

If you do this, everyone will know that you are my friends and God's friends too."

PEACE (based on John 14:27)

Jesus said,

"Peace I give to you.

My own peace I leave with you.

A peace which no one else can offer, this is my gift to you.

Don't ever let your hearts be troubled or afraid.

My gift to you is my peace."

How do you think Jesus' friends felt when they heard these things?

What have you read that helps you?

Gospels

REMAIN IN MY LOVE (based on John 15:9-14)

I love you in the same way as the Father loves me. My love for you never changes. Remain in my love.

I have kept my Father's commandments and remain in his love. If you do the same and keep my commandments, you will remain in my love.

I am telling you this because I want to be full of joy for you and I want you to be full of joy for me.

This is my commandment, "Love one another in the same way as I love you. The greatest love a person can have for his friends is to give up his life for them. You are my friends if you do what I command you."

THE PROMISE OF THE SPIRIT (based on John 16:5,7,13)

Jesus said, "I am going back to my Father who sent me. It is better for you if I go away. If I go, I will be able to send someone else to help you – the Holy Spirit of truth. The Holy Spirit will guide and lead you. The Holy Spirit will help you to understand all the things I have done and everything that I have said to you. He will teach you everything that I have learned from my Father. The Holy Spirit will help you to know how you are to live, now and in the future."

JESUS' PRAYER FOR HIS FRIENDS (based on John 17:11-12; 20-23)

"Holy Father, I am coming to you.

Keep my friends safe.

They belong to you.

Keep them close to you and to each other.

Let them be as close as I am to you.

I kept them close to you."

"Father, I pray for these my friends
and for all those in the future whom they will bring to know me.

Just as you and I are one,
I pray that my friends will always be one with us and with one another.

I pray that they will be so at one with one another,
that everyone will know that you sent me,
and that you have loved them as you have loved me."

Gospels

The True Vine

Jesus often used the things people did every day to help us to understand what he was teaching. He spoke about the fishermen casting their nets, a farmer sowing his field, a mother mending clothes, a person losing something precious. He spoke about ordinary, little things like birds, seeds, plants and coins.

On one occasion he used an ordinary vine, growing on the wall of a house, to explain how very close he wants to be to us, how he shares his own life with us and how we can grow closer to him.

If you hold a bunch of grapes, you can easily see how each grape is joined by its tiny stem to a bigger stem, and you can trace it right back to the main stem of the vine. Each grape draws its sap, the food which gives it life, directly from the main vine itself. If you pull off a grape or cut off a bunch, it will soon wither and die. Shops have to be sure to sell the grapes very quickly once they reach the market.

The vine-grower knows quite well that if he wants good grapes he must feed the root-stock, keep it well dug around and watered, particularly during the hot, dry weather. The grapes will become full and sweet and beautiful to see and taste if he cares for the vine.

Now you can see what Jesus was trying to say to his friends at the last supper.

Gospels

I AM THE TRUE VINE (based on John 15:1-12)

"I am the true vine, and my Father is the vinedresser. A branch cannot bear fruit all by itself, but must remain part of the vine, neither can you bear fruit unless you remain in me. I am the vine; you are the branches. Whoever remains in me, with me in him, bears fruit in plenty; for cut off from me you can do nothing. Anyone who does not remain in me is like a branch that has been thrown away, he withers.

As the Father has loved me, so I have loved you. **Remain in my love.** If you keep my commandments, you will remain in my love. This is my commandment: love one another, as I have loved you."

'Remain in my love': other translations have 'Make your home in me' or 'abide in my love.': Jesus is saying that having a close relationship with God is very important. It is what he has come to invite everyone to have.

Gospels

THE GREATEST WEEK

For the Church, 'the greatest week' is Holy Week when the death and resurrection of Jesus are remembered in special celebrations. Holy Week begins on Passion Sunday, also called Palm Sunday, and ends on Easter Sunday.

All four evangelists tell the story of the passion and death of Jesus, but each adds details that highlight each one's message about Jesus.

You will read the story as it is told in the Gospel of **Mark** and learn about the details added by the other gospels: **Matthew:** The Great Darkness, **Luke:** Jesus is sent to Herod; The Two Thieves, **John:** The Washing of the Feet; Jesus and his Mother.

FROM DEATH TO LIFE

(based on John 12:24-25)

Jesus said: A grain of wheat is only one grain unless it falls into the ground and dies. If it does this, the one grain will grow into many grains. It's the same with people. If you only take great care of yourself, you will become selfish and end up on your own. But if you are kind and giving, thinking only of others, then your life will be fruitful for yourself and others.

The Greatest Week

THE TIME IS NEAR (based on John 12:1-11)

Six days before the Passover feast, Jesus went to Bethany where Lazarus lived. There they had a dinner for Jesus. Martha served the food and Lazarus was among those at the table. Mary brought in half-a-litre of very expensive perfume. She poured the perfume on Jesus' feet, and then she wiped his feet with her long hair. The sweet smell of the perfume filled the whole house. Judas Iscariot, one of Jesus' followers, the one who would betray him said, "This perfume is worth a lot of money. Why wasn't it sold and the money given to the poor?"

Judas didn't really care about the poor. He said this because he was a thief. He was the one in charge of the money, and he often stole some of it and kept it for himself.

Jesus answered, "Leave her alone. She wanted to show me respect. The poor will be with you always. I won't always be here."

Mark's story

PALM SUNDAY (based on Mark 11: 1-11)

As Jesus and his disciples were getting close to Jerusalem, they came to the Mount of Olives. He sent two of his disciples on ahead of the others with these instructions, "Go into the village you see ahead of you. As you enter it, you will find a colt tied up, that no one has ever ridden. Untie it and bring it to me. If anyone asks you what you are doing, say, 'The Master needs it and will send it back at once'." They went off and did as Jesus said. They brought the colt to Jesus and threw their cloaks on its back. Jesus mounted the colt. Lots of people spread their cloaks on the road, while others cut branches and spread these before him. The people who walked in front and those who followed on behind were all shouting, "Hosanna! Praise God! Blessed is he who comes in the name of the Lord! Hosanna! Praise God!

The Greatest Week

HOLY THURSDAY (based on Mark 14: 12-16)

On the first day of Feast of the Unleavened Bread Jesus' disciples asked him, "Where do you want us to go and prepare the Passover Meal for you?" So he sent two of his disciples, saying to them, "Go into the city. A man carrying a jug of water will meet you there. Follow him to the house he enters. Say to the owner of that house, 'The Master says, where is the room where my disciples and I will eat the Passover Meal?' He will show you a large upstairs room all prepared and furnished with couches. Get everything ready for us there."

The disciples left, went into the city and found everything just as Jesus had told them. They prepared the Passover Meal.

THE LAST SUPPER (based on Mark 14:22-25)

In the evening Jesus and the twelve came to the supper room.

During the meal, Jesus took some bread, blessed it and gave it to them. "Take this," he said, "This is my body."

Then he took a cup of wine, said the blessing and gave it to them and they all drank from the cup. He said to them, "This is my blood, the blood of the covenant, which will be poured out for everyone."

The Greatest Week

Peter did not want Jesus to wash his feet. He did not understand what Jesus was teaching his friends.

From John's Gospel (based on John 13:4-9, 12-15)

Just before they began their last supper together, Jesus wrapped a towel around himself, filled a bowl of water and knelt before each one of them to wash their feet and wipe them with the towel.

Peter was horrified and tried to refuse. "You shall never wash my feet, " he said. This was the service done by the lowest of all the slaves.

Then Jesus told him, "If I do not wash you, you cannot share my life."

At this, Peter said, "Then, Lord, wash not only my feet but also my hands and my head."

When he had finished, Jesus explained exactly what his action meant.

"Do you understand," he said, "what I have done for you? You call me Master and Lord, and rightly; so I am. If I then, the Lord and Master, have washed your feet, you should wash each other's feet. I have given you an example so that you may copy what I have done for you."

The Greatest Week

A Problem for Peter (based on Mark 14:26-31)

After they had finished supper, Jesus and his disciples set out for the Mount of Olives. Jesus said, "You will all run away and leave me."

Peter said, "Even if everyone else runs away I will never leave you."

Jesus said, "I'm telling you, three times tonight before the cock crows twice, you will say you do not know me."

Peter protested, saying, "I will die before I deny you."

And the other disciples said the same.

Gethsemane (based on Mark 14:32-46)

When they reached the place called Gethsemane, Jesus said to his apostles, "Sit here while I go over there to pray."

He took Peter, James and John with him. He was very frightened, and he said to them, "My heart is ready to break. I'm so terrified of what is going to happen to me. You wait here and stay awake."

He went a little further on, threw himself on the ground and prayed. "Father," he said, "You can do anything. Take this suffering from me. But I will do what you want, not what I want."

He came back and found his friends asleep, and he said to Peter, "Simon are you asleep? Could you not stay awake even for one hour? Stay awake and pray."

He went away once more and prayed saying the same words. Then he came back and found them asleep again. They could not keep their eyes open, and they did not know what to say to him.

When he came back a third time, he said to them, "You can sleep on now and have your rest. The hour has come. I am going to be betrayed and handed over to violent people. Get up! Let us go! My betrayer is not very far away."

He was still speaking when Judas, one of the twelve apostles came with some soldiers. They were armed with swords and sticks. They had been sent by the chief priests, the teachers of the law and the elders. Judas had said to them, 'The one I kiss is the one you want. Arrest him and make sure he is well guarded as you lead him away'.

As soon as Judas arrived, he went up to Jesus and said, "Rabbi," and kissed him.

Then they took hold of Jesus and arrested him.

The Greatest Week

Ancient olive trees in the garden at Gethsemane.

The Greatest Week

GOOD FRIDAY (based on Mark 15:1-15)

Early in the morning, the chief priests, the elders, the teachers of the law and the whole council had their plan ready. They tied Jesus' hands and led him away to hand him over to **Pilate**. Pilate asked him, "Are you the King of the Jews?"

Jesus said, "The words are yours."

The chief priests were accusing Jesus of all sorts of things, so Pilate asked him again, "Aren't you going to say anything? Listen to all they are saying about you."

Again, Jesus refused to say a word, and Pilate was amazed.

At every Passover festival, Pilate usually set free one prisoner. At that time a man named Barabbas was in prison. He had committed a murder during a riot. When the crowd gathered Pilate asked, "Do you want me to set the King of the Jews free or Barabbas?"

He knew that the chief priests had handed Jesus over because they were jealous of him. But the chief priests stirred up the crowd and got them to ask for Barabbas to be set free.

Pilate spoke again to the crowd, "What do you want me to do with the man you call the King of the Jews?"

They shouted back, "Crucify him!"

"But what crime has he committed?" Pilate asked.

They shouted all the louder, "Crucify him!"

Pilate wanted to please the crowd, so he set Barabbas free for them. Then he had Jesus **whipped** and handed him over to be crucified.

THE SOLDIERS (based on Mark 15:16-21)

The soldiers took Jesus away to the inner part of the palace, the Praetorium and called together the rest of the company.

They put a **purple robe** on Jesus, twisted some thorns into a crown and put it on him. Then they began to salute him saying, "Hail King of the Jews!"

They beat him over the head with a stick and spat on him. They went down on their knees and bowed to him.

When they had finished making fun of him, they took off the purple robe and put his own clothes back on him. Then they led him out to crucify him.

The Greatest Week

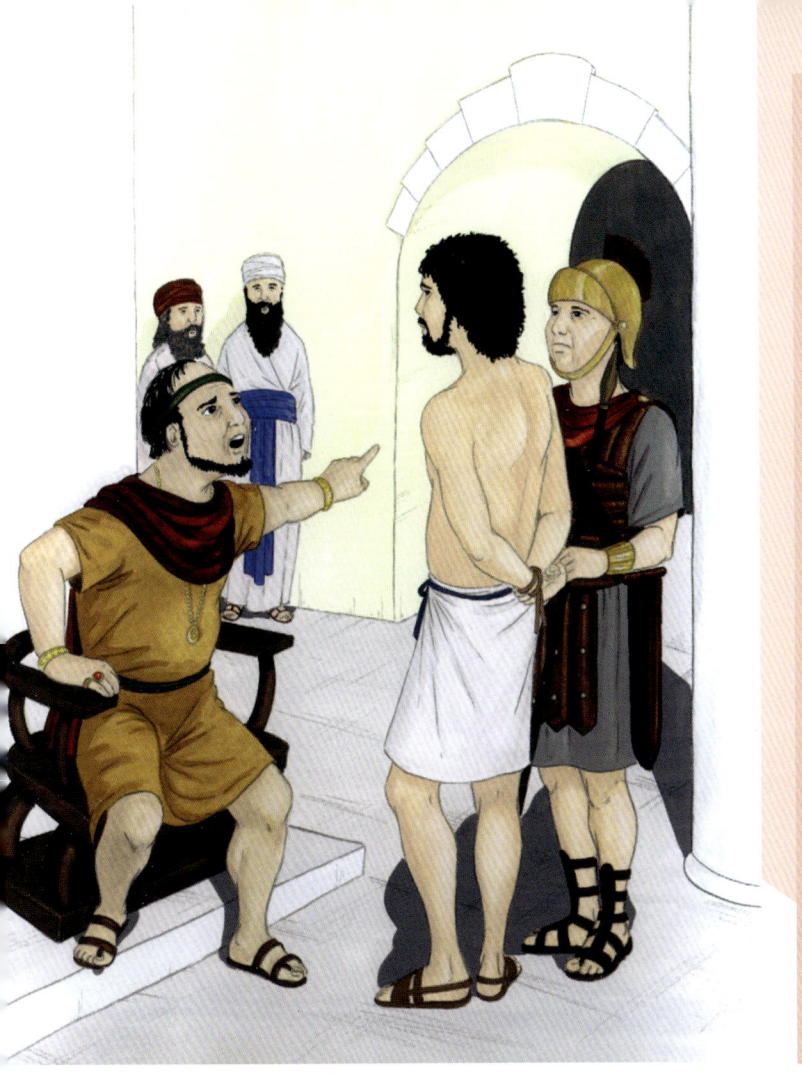

Pilate

The Romans ruled Palestine, and Pilate was the governor appointed by the Roman emperor. The Jewish council did not have the power to condemn someone to death, so they had to go to the Roman governor. Pilate tried to please the crowd because he did not want bad reports of him to get back to Rome.

whipped

This was often done to weaken prisoners before they were put to death. Another word for 'whipped' is 'scourged'.

a purple robe

This was a symbol of a king.

What else did the soldiers do that were signs of kingship?

From Luke's Gospel

JESUS IS SENT TO HEROD (based on Luke 22:6-12)

When Pilate found out that Jesus was from Galilee, he sent him to King Herod.

Herod had heard about Jesus and for a long time had wanted to meet him, because he wanted to see a miracle. He questioned Jesus for a long time, but Jesus would not answer.

Then Herod and all his royal court mocked Jesus and made fun of him. Herod put a cloak of royal purple on him and sent him back to Pilate.

The Greatest Week

ON THE WAY TO CALVARY (based on Mark 15: 21-27)

On the way, they met a man named Simon, from Cyrene. He was the father of Alexander and Rufus. He was coming into the city from the country, and the soldiers forced him to carry Jesus' cross.

They took Jesus to a place called Golgotha, which means the place of the skull. There they tried to give him wine, mixed with **myrrh**, but Jesus would not drink it. Then they crucified him and divided his clothes among themselves. They threw dice to decide what each should get.

It was nine o'clock in the morning when they **crucified** him. The notice above his head said, '**Jesus of Nazareth, the King of the Jews.**'

Two thieves were crucified at the same time. One was on his right side, and the other on his left.

The Greatest Week

THE THIEVES (based on Luke 23: 26-43)

The soldiers led Jesus away. On the road, they met a man called Simon. He came from Cyrene. He was on his way from the country into the city. They forced him to carry the cross behind Jesus. A large crowd of people went after them. Among them were women who cried when they saw Jesus. Jesus turned to them and said, "Do not weep for me. Weep for yourselves, and for your children."

Jesus was nailed to a cross outside the city walls. There were two others put to death with him, one on his right and the other on his left. When Jesus was dying, he said, "Father forgive them. They do not know that they are doing."

The soldiers played a game of dice to decide who would have his clothes. There was a notice nailed to the cross of Jesus. It said, "This is Jesus of Nazareth, the King of the Jews!"

One of the men on the cross made fun of Jesus saying, "If you are a real king, why don't you save us all?"

The other man told him to be quiet because Jesus had done nothing wrong. Then he said to Jesus, "Please remember me. Don't ever forget me."

Jesus said, "I will remember you today, and you will be with me always."

Myrrh
A pain-killing drug given to a condemned man to help deaden the pain.

Crucified
To nail to a wooden cross. Criminals were crucified.

Jesus of Nazareth, the King of the Jews
Sometimes you will see the letters INRI on a crucifix. These are the first letters of the Latin words which mean 'Jesus of Nazareth, the King of the Jews'. (Iesus Nazarenus Rex Iudaeorum)

The Greatest Week

The Death of Jesus

(based on Mark 15:21-41)

People passing by insulted Jesus. They shook their heads and said, "Come down from the cross and save yourself."

The chief priests and the teachers of the law jeered at Jesus, saying to each other, "He saved others, but he cannot save himself. Let the Christ, the King of Israel, come down from the cross now, and we will believe in him."

The two who were crucified with him insulted him too. At midday the whole country became dark. This lasted three hours.

At three o'clock, Jesus cried out, "**Eloi, Eloi Lama Sabactani**," which means, 'My God, my God, why have you abandoned me?'

Some of the people there heard him and said, "Listen, he is calling for **Elijah**."

Someone soaked a sponge in cheap wine and put it on the end of a stick. He held it to his lips saying, "Let's see if Elijah will come and take him down from the cross."

Then Jesus gave a loud cry and died.

When the **centurion**, who was standing opposite saw how he died, he said, "This man really was the Son of God."

Some women were there watching from a distance. They were Mary of Magdala, Mary, the Mother of the younger James and of Joseph, and Salome. They had followed Jesus and had helped him when he was in Galilee. Many other women were there who had come up to Jerusalem with him.

The Greatest Week

From John's Gospel
JESUS AND HIS MOTHER

(based on John 19:25-27)

Mary, the mother of Jesus, stood beside the cross of her dying son. Her sister was with her and so was Mary of Magdala, and Mary, the wife of Cleopas.

Jesus said to his mother, "My friend will now be your son. Take care of him."

Then he said to his dear friend, "Mary will be your Mother now."

When Jesus died, this friend took Mary home with him.

From Matthew's Gospel
THE GREAT DARKNESS

(based on Matthew 27:45, 51, 54)

From the sixth hour, there was a great darkness over the land until the ninth hour. At the same moment, as Jesus cried out and died, the veil of the Temple was torn in two from top to bottom. There was an earthquake and rocks were split.

The centurion and the soldiers who were guarding Jesus were terrified and said, "It's true. This man was a son of God."

Eloi, Eloi, lama sabachthani
The first words of Psalm 22 in Hebrew. Do you remember that this psalm begins with a cry of despair and ends in a prayer of trust? Look back to p.45.

Elijah
The great prophet the Jewish people expected to return to them to prepare the way for God's Promised One.

centurion
A Roman officer in charge of one hundred men.

The Sorrowful Mysteries
The Agony in the Garden
The Scourging
The Crowning with Thorns
The Carrying of the Cross
The Crucifixion

These events of the passion and death of Jesus make up the Sorrowful Mysteries of the Rosary. The Rosary is a prayer. People ask Mary, the mother of Jesus, to help them to remember the life of Jesus and come to know him better.

The Greatest Week

THE BURIAL OF JESUS (based on Mark 15: 42-47)

It was nearly evening. Since it was Preparation Day, that is, the day before the Sabbath, Joseph of Arimathaea went boldly to Pilate and asked for the body of Jesus. Joseph was an important and respected member of the Council.

Pilate was astonished to hear that Jesus was already dead. He sent for the centurion and asked how long he had been dead. When he heard the centurion's report, Pilate told Joseph that he could have the body.

Joseph brought a linen sheet, took the body down from the cross and wrapped it in the sheet. He laid it in a **tomb**, which had been carved out of solid rock. Then he rolled a stone against the entrance to the tomb.

Mary of Magdala and Mary, the mother of Joseph, were watching and made note of the place where Jesus was laid.

tomb

A cave carved out of rock and used as a grave, not a hole dug in the ground.

The Greatest Week

THE EMPTY TOMB

All four evangelists tell the story of the Sunday morning and the empty tomb. As you read their stories, notice where they agree and what is different in each account. What is the important message they all want to give?

Mark's Story (based on Mark 16:2-8)

Very early on Sunday morning, Mary of Magdala, Mary the mother of James, and Salome went to Jesus' tomb. The sun was just coming up.

They had been asking one another about who would roll away the heavy stone across the entrance, but as they came close, they could see it had been moved already. As they went into the tomb, they saw a young man dressed in white sitting there. They were amazed.

He said to them, "Don't be afraid. I know you are looking for Jesus who was crucified. He is risen; he is not here. See, here's the place where his body was laid. But you must go and tell Peter and his disciples that Jesus is going to Galilee. You will see him, just as he told you."

The women came out. They ran away because they were still frightened, and said nothing to anyone because they were afraid.

A tomb in the rock – Jesus was buried in a grave like this.

He is risen : he is not here

The Empty Tomb

Matthew's Story

(based on Matthew 28:1-10)

After the Sabbath, very early on Sunday morning, Mary of Magdala and the other Mary went to look at the tomb. Suddenly there was a violent earthquake. An angel of the Lord came and rolled away the stone and sat on it. His face was lit up, and his clothes were as white as snow. The guards were so afraid that they trembled and could not do anything.

The angel spoke to the women, "Do not be afraid. I know you are looking for Jesus, who was crucified. He is not here. He has been raised from death. Come and see the place where he lay, and then go quickly and tell his disciples that he is risen from the dead and is going ahead of you to Galilee. You will see him there." Filled with deep wonder and great joy the women ran to tell the disciples.

Suddenly, Jesus was there, coming to meet them. "Peace be with you," he said. The women went up to him, took hold of his feet and bowed down and worshipped him. Then Jesus said to them, "Do not be afraid; go and tell my brothers that they must go to Galilee; they will see me there."

Luke's Story (based on Luke 24:1-12)

Very early on Sunday morning, just as the sun was beginning to rise, the women went to the tomb. They took with them spices that they had prepared. They found that the stone had been rolled away from the tomb. They went in but could not find the body of the Lord Jesus. As they stood there puzzling over this, two men in bright shining clothes appeared at their side. The women were terrified and bowed down to the ground. The two men said to them, "Why are you looking among the dead for someone who is alive? He is not here; he has been raised from the dead."

The women returned from the tomb and told all this to the Eleven, and to the other disciples. The women were Mary of Magdala, Joanna and Mary the mother of James. They and the other women with them told all these things to the apostles. But the apostles thought that what the women said was nonsense, and they did not believe them.

The Empty Tomb

JOHN'S STORY (based on John 20: 1-10)

Very early, on the first day of the week, while it was still dark, Mary of Magdala went to the tomb She saw that the stone had been moved away from the entrance to the tomb. She went running to tell Simon Peter and the other disciple, the one whom Jesus loved. She said to them, "They have taken the Lord from the tomb. We do not know where they have put him."

Peter and the other disciple went to the tomb. They both ran, but the other disciple ran faster than Peter and got there first. He bent down and saw the linen cloths lying on the ground, but he did not go in. Simon Peter came up behind him and went into the tomb. He saw the linen cloths lying on the ground as well as the cloth that had been around Jesus' head. This was not with the other linen cloths but was rolled up in a place by itself. Then the other disciple, who had reached the tomb first, also went in. He saw and believed. The disciples then went back home.

The Empty Tomb

NEW LIFE: A NEW BEGINNING

The friends of Jesus could not believe what had happened. They were devastated when Jesus died, and they were slow to believe that he was truly alive. The gospel stories show this. Jesus is the same and yet different. They are terrified and delighted.

ON THE ROAD TO EMMAUS

(based on Luke 24:13-35)

On the Sunday evening, two disciples were on their way to Emmaus, a village seven miles from Jerusalem. They were talking about everything that had happened and did not recognise the stranger who joined them as they walked along.

"What are you talking about so sadly?" he asked them.

They turned to him, their faces full of their sadness. The disciple named Cleopas answered him. "You must be the only person in Jerusalem who does not know all the things that have been going on these last few days?"

"What things?" Jesus asked.

"What happened to Jesus of Nazareth," they said, "the great prophet who showed by all he did and said that he was sent by God. Our chief priests and leaders handed him over to the Romans, and he was crucified. We had hoped that he was the Promised One who would set Israel free. This morning, some women went to the tomb where he had been buried and came back saying they had seen a vision of angels and that Jesus was alive. Some of our friends went to the tomb and found it empty as the women had said, but they didn't see anything of Jesus."

Jesus said to them, "How slow you are to believe! Don't you remember the promises of the prophets about the Christ who would suffer and rise to new life?"

They told their story, and how they recognised him in the breaking of bread.

New Life: A New Beginning

Then Jesus started with Moses and went through all the Scriptures explaining the message about himself.

By now they were near to Emmaus, and they begged him to stay with them. So he did, and they sat down at table together. He took the bread, blessed it and broke it and gave it to them. Suddenly, as if their eyes had just opened, they recognised him; but even as they did, he vanished.

"How could we not have known!" they exclaimed. "Weren't our hearts burning as he talked to us and explained the Scriptures to us?"

At once they set out and returned to Jerusalem. When they arrived, the Eleven and the other disciples said, "Yes, it's true! He has appeared to Simon!" and then they told their story and how they had recognised him when he blessed and broke the bread.

New Life: A New Beginning

JESUS APPEARS TO HIS FRIENDS (based on Luke 24:36-49)

The friends of Jesus were gathered together talking about their experiences. Jesus stood among them and said, "Peace be with you." They were terrified. They thought they were seeing a ghost. "Why are you worried?" asked Jesus. "Why do you doubt? Look at my hands and my feet. It is really I. Touch me. You can't touch a ghost." He showed them his hands and his feet. They were delighted, but they still couldn't believe it. "Have you got anything to eat?" asked Jesus. They gave him a piece of grilled fish. They watched him eat it.

Jesus explained the meaning of the Scriptures to them once again so that they could really understand. "You know the Scriptures say that God's chosen leader would die but that he would rise again. You must tell everyone. Begin in Jerusalem. Tell them that if they change their ways, God will forgive them for all the wrong things they have done. You know this is true. I will give you what God my Father promised – God's own power in your hearts. Stay here in this city until this happens."

GO OUT ALL OVER THE WORLD (based on Matthew 28:16-20)

The eleven disciples set out for Galilee, to the mountain where Jesus had said he would meet them. When they saw him, they knelt down before him. Jesus said to them, "My Father has given me power in heaven and on earth. Go all over the whole world. Make disciples of all the peoples. Baptise them, in the name of the Father and of the Son and of the Holy Spirit. Teach everyone to live as I have taught you how to live; show everyone how to love as I have shown you how to love. Remember my promise. I am with you always, close by, ready to help. Yes, forever, until the very end of time."

New Life: A New Beginning

THE ACTS OF THE APOSTLES

This is Luke's second book. He wrote it for someone called Theophilus. He begins with the mission Jesus gave his disciples and how the Holy Spirit came just as Jesus had promised. The rest of the book tells of the adventures of some of the people who took the Good News of Jesus to the peoples of the world.

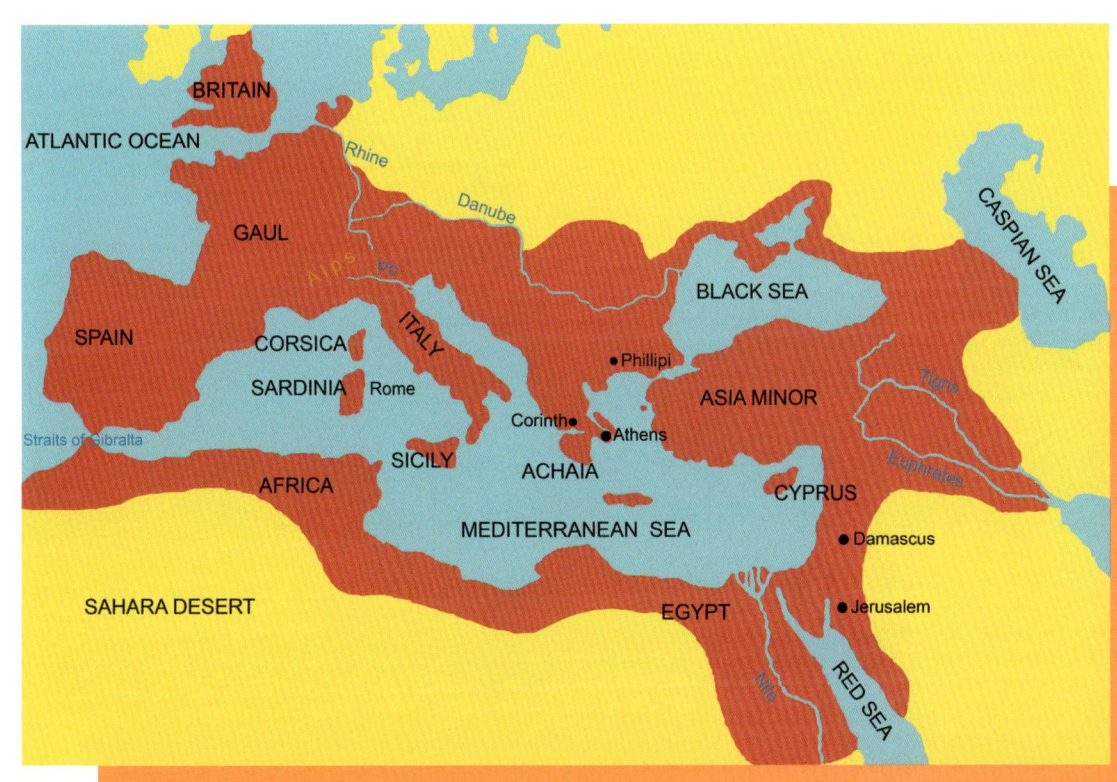

Rome was the centre of the world – Romans were the superpower. This map shows the extent of the Roman empire.

You will be my witnesses all over the world.

The Acts of the Apostles

THE ASCENSION (based on Acts 1:6-11)

After Jesus had been raised to new life, he told his friends, "You will receive the power of the Holy Spirit. You will be my witnesses here in Jerusalem and all over the world." As he said this, he disappeared from sight. They realised that he had gone back to his Father as he had said he would.

PENTECOST (based on Acts 2: 1-43)

When the harvest was being gathered in, on the feast of the first fruits, the friends of Jesus were not among the holiday crowds celebrating **Pentecost** in Jerusalem. Instead, they were hidden away in a quiet room. Mary, the Mother of Jesus, was with them.

> How do you think the friends of Jesus felt when he asked them to take his message out to all the world?
>
> How would you have felt?
>
> Who spreads this message today? Do you? How?

Without the warmth of Jesus' presence among them, they felt stranded and clueless. When Jesus had walked and talked with them, their hearts had burned within them; but now there was a death-like stillness and silence within them, which chilled their hearts and froze their power to act.

Then on that Pentecost morning, everything changed. The friends of Jesus knew all would be well.

They described the experience like this. They said it was as if a strong, powerful wind had filled the whole house and as if tongues of fire had spread out and touched each one of them. They felt alive as never before. The warmth of God's love circulated through and among them so that they felt compelled to rush out and share their joy with the whole world and to witness to the Good News of Jesus.

No longer tongue-tied, but with fiery conviction, the words tumbled out so fast and free, that, in their excitement, they sounded crazy, as if they'd lost their senses. At first, people thought they were drunk.

It was Peter who controlled the situation; no longer afraid, he told the crowds how God had generously poured out the Spirit upon all so that they could speak out. A great change took place amidst the listening crowds.

The Acts of the Apostles

Barriers between people seemed to be melting away, barriers of language disappeared, so that everyone understood and heard what he or she most needed to hear. The love of God for people was 'like a flash of fire, a flame of Yahweh Himself', burning away all the rubbish in their lives, and leaving behind only what was firm and strong and for good.

The good news of God's love and power spread like sparks from a mighty fire and warmed the people's hearts towards God and all peoples.

The Spirit was with them, and so they could share their lives together in peace. Onlookers cried out in astonishment: "See how these Christians love one another!" And the Spirit watched over the dawning of a new creation, a whole new way of living.

Pentecost
A Greek word meaning fiftieth. This Jewish 'feast of weeks' was held fifty days after the beginning of the grain harvest. It was a thanksgiving feast.

The Glorious Mysteries
The Resurrection, The Ascension of Jesus and The Coming of the Holy Spirit are the first three Glorious Mysteries of the Rosary.

The Acts of the Apostles

WE ARE WITNESSES (based on Acts 2:22-24,32)

Peter stood up with the other eleven apostles and spoke in a loud voice to the huge crowd who had gathered.

"Listen everyone to what I am going to say. Jesus of Nazareth was sent to you by God. He lived among you and did many good and wonderful works for you, as you know. You took him and had him crucified. You killed him, but God the Father raised him to new life.

We know he is alive for we have seen him.

We are his witnesses."

THE NEW PEOPLE OF GOD (based on Acts 2:43-47; 4:32-37)

Many people joined the community of the friends of Jesus. They lived every day as they were taught. They lived like members of one big family. They ate together sharing bread and wine as Jesus had done at the Last Supper. They prayed together often.

Everyone was amazed at the life they lived. The apostles did wonderful work among the people.

The community of friends shared everything with one another. They sold everything they owned and shared out the money so that each person had what they needed.

Every day they went together to the temple. Every day they met in their houses to break bread together. They happily shared their food with each other, praising God with joy. People were very impressed with the way they lived. Day by day, more people joined them.

They were totally together as a group. None of them kept anything they owned just for themselves. Everything was shared. The close friends of Jesus continued to tell people of Jesus' new life, and everyone treated them with great respect.

They were a happy community. No one ever had to go without. Those who owned land or houses would even sell them and bring the money to the group. The apostles would give it to those who needed it. There was a man called Joseph from Cyprus who sold his piece of land and gave the money to the apostles. They gave him a new surname: Barnabas. This means 'one who supports'.

The Acts of the Apostles

They were a happy community.

They were totally together as a group.

The Acts of the Apostles

WE CANNOT KEEP SILENT (based on Acts 4:1-26)

The friends of Jesus were full of new life and could not stop telling everyone about Jesus. Their minds and hearts were full of all he had done and said. When they went to the temple to pray, they talked to people and crowds gathered around them. They helped the poor and the sick.

Some of the officials in the temple were very annoyed about everything that was happening. One day they had Peter and John arrested and put them in prison.

The next day all the council officials assembled and had Peter and John brought before them. "We've heard that you are going about preaching about Jesus and healing. What right do you have to do this?" they asked.

Peter and John were not afraid, "Whatever good we do," said Peter, "we do in the name of Jesus Christ of Nazareth. You crucified him, but God raised him from the dead."

The whole council were amazed that two very ordinary men were not afraid, and were able to speak out boldly. They discussed the matter and then ordered the disciples never to speak or teach in the name of Jesus.

But Peter and John were not frightened by any of their threats and said, "We cannot keep silent about the great things that God has done. We have to spread the Good News of Jesus."

The officials had to let them go because the people were so glad about what they were doing, and the officials did not want to risk a riot.

When Peter and John got back to the other disciples, everyone thanked God for their safety and the courage that the coming of the Holy Spirit had given them.

The Acts of the Apostles

Sharing the Mission (based on Acts 6:2-13; 7: 57-60)

The twelve apostles called a meeting of all Jesus' friends.

They said: "More and more people want to hear the Good News. It is important that we give as much time as we can to telling people about Jesus. We need help to give out the food. Then we can spend more time teaching and praying. Please choose from among you seven good people to help."

The friends of Jesus agreed and picked seven. One of the seven was Stephen. The apostles laid their hands on the seven and prayed for them. The apostles spread the Good News to many more people, and these became followers of Jesus.

Good news for everyone.

The Acts of the Apostles

STEPHEN (based on Acts 6:6 -7:6)

Stephen, filled with the power of God's Spirit, did marvellous work among the Jewish people in Jerusalem who had come from North Africa and Asia. Many of them were in Jerusalem on pilgrimage. Some of them tried to argue with Stephen, but they found it too difficult. Stephen was very wise, and the Holy Spirit was with him. They were angry and told lies about Stephen.

They turned the scribes and elders against him as well as some of the people. Stephen was arrested. When Stephen stood up in court, he spoke for a long time about the ways in which they had refused to listen to God, and to God's messengers.

He told the judge and the people about Jesus, but they did not want to listen. They put their hands over their ears. Then they charged at him and dragged him outside the city. There they threw stones at him until he was dead. A young man called Saul watched. He was taking care of their cloaks. Before he died Stephen said: "Lord Jesus, receive my spirit. Do not blame them for what they have done."

IN SAMARIA (based on Acts 8:14-17)

The apostles in Jerusalem heard that the people in Samaria had received the Good News, so they sent Peter and John to them. When Peter and John arrived, they laid hands on those who had been baptised in the name of Jesus, and they received the Holy Spirit.

PHILIP AND THE ETHIOPIAN OFFICIAL (based on Acts 8:26-30, 34-38)

Philip was a follower of Jesus. One day he went walking on the desert road from Jerusalem to Gaza. A chariot passed him. In it was an officer of the court of the Queen of Ethiopia. This man was reading one of the books of the Bible: the book of the prophet Isaiah.

God's Spirit spoke to Philip, saying, "Go to meet that chariot."

When he reached the chariot, Philip heard the Ethiopian reading the words of Isaiah: "Do you understand what you are reading?" asked Philip. "How can I understand unless I have someone to help me?" he replied.

He asked Philip to help him.

"Come up here beside me," he said. Philip did as he asked.

The Acts of the Apostles

The Ethiopian said, "Who is this prophet talking about here?" Philip explained that the passage was about Jesus and went on to tell him more of the Good News of Jesus.

A little further on they saw some water, and the Ethiopian asked, "Is there anything to stop me being baptised?"

He stopped the chariot. Philip went down with him into the water and baptised him, there and then.

The Ethiopian continued his journey rejoicing. Philip went on telling the Good News everywhere he went.

PAUL, LUKE AND TIMOTHY MEET LYDIA (based on Acts 16:11-15)

We took a ship from Troas and sailed to Samothrace. The next day we went on to Neapolis and from there sailed inland to Philippi. It is **a Roman colony** and the most important city in Macedonia. We spent a few days here. On the Sabbath, we went outside the city gates to a place by the river where the Jews gathered to pray. We sat down and talked to the women who had come there. One of them was called Lydia. She was from Thyatira and was in the business of dying and selling **purple cloth**. She loved and worshipped God and listened carefully to us. God opened her mind and heart to believe what Paul said. After she and all the people who lived in her house had been baptised, she invited us to stay with them.

a Roman colony

Paul was a Roman citizen and could travel freely all over the Roman Empire, which, at that time, included Greece and Egypt.

purple cloth

Purple cloth was fashionable so Lydia was probably a successful trader and may have been well known in the city.

The friends of Jesus preached the good news in the marketplace or wherever people gathered.

The Acts of the Apostles

SPREADING THE GOOD NEWS

We have some of the letters the apostles wrote. In these, they spread the good news of Jesus and teach new Christians how they in their turn can do the same.

Greetings to the Church in…

Spreading the Good News

From Paul's Letter to the Romans

GOD IS FOR US (based on Romans 8:28,31-32,34-39)

We know that no matter what happens
God is working for the good with those who love God.

What else can we say?

If God is for us, who can be against us?

Not God certainly, for God gave us Jesus, his only Son.

Not Jesus either for he died for us, was raised to life
and is now with the Father praying for us.

Who then can separate us from the love of Jesus?

Can trouble? Or hard times? Or persecution? Or hunger?

Or poverty?

Or even death itself?

No! God is always there, no matter what is happening.

I am sure that nothing can separate us from God's love:
neither death nor life,
neither what is happening now nor what will happen in the future.

There is nothing that will ever be able to separate us from the love of God which is ours through Christ Jesus our Lord.

BE REAL ABOUT LOVING (based on Romans 12:8-11)

Dear Friends

We all have been given lovely gifts.

When you give, give with a loving heart.

If you have a job to do, do it really well.

If you are helping someone, do it happily.

Be real in your love for each other.

Do not just pretend to be good.

Love and care for each other
as good brothers and sisters.

Be wholehearted and enthusiastic in all you do.

Be joyful.

When things get hard, keep on going.

Pray regularly.

Share what you have with people in need.

Always make people feel welcome.

Spreading the Good News

JESUS CAME FOR EVERYONE (based on Romans 15:4-9)

Everything that was written long ago in the Scriptures
was written to encourage us,
to help us never to give up,
to teach us something about hope.

May the God of patience and encouragement
who helps you when you refuse to give up,
grant you the gift of living in peace and harmony
with one another,
so that you may together give glory
to the God and Father of Our Lord Jesus Christ
with one heart and one voice.

Jesus was born into the Jewish people.

He lived and worked among them
to help those people realise how faithful God is.

He wanted them to see how much God
had done for them
right from the earliest days,
to show them that God kept the promises
made to their ancestors.

He came not only for the Jewish people
but for people all over the world,
so that they too might know God's love and care for them.

Then everyone could give praise and glory
for God's mercy and faithful love.

Paul and Peter took the good news to Rome. Today, the Vatican is home for St Peter's successor, the Pope.

Spreading the Good News

From Paul's letters to the Corinthians

What I heard I am handing on (based on 1 Corinthians 11:24-27)

The tradition that I received is one which goes right back to Jesus himself. It is this same tradition which I have handed on to you: that on the night he was betrayed, the Lord Jesus, took some bread, gave thanks to God, broke the bread and said, This is my body which is for you, do this in remembrance of me."

Then, in the same way, he took the cup of wine after supper, gave thanks to God and said, "This cup is the cup of my life blood, whenever you drink it do this as a memorial of me."

This means that whenever you eat this bread and drink this cup, you are proclaiming the death of Jesus until he comes.

Love (based on 1 Corinthians 12:31, 13:1-8)

If you are the cleverest person on earth but do not love, you are nothing.

If you give away everything you possess but do not love, it will do you no good.

Love is always patient and kind.

It is never jealous.

Love is never boastful or conceited.

It is never rude or selfish.

It does not take offence and is not resentful.

Love takes no pleasure in other people's sins, but delights in the truth.

It is always ready to excuse, to trust, to hope and to endure whatever comes.

Love does not come to an end.

All the wonderful and clever things that people can say and do will come to an end.

Love never ends.

Spreading the Good News

Paul's Happiness (based on 2 Corinthians 6:3-10)

I've had to put up with all sorts of things – dangers and hard times and all sorts of difficulties; I've been flogged, put in prison and beaten up; I've had to work like a slave, go without sleep and food.

People have sometimes honoured me, and sometimes insulted me; sometimes praised me, and sometimes blamed me. They thought I was lying, yet I always tried to tell the truth; they called me a nobody, yet everybody knew me; my life wasn't worth living, yet I have enjoyed every moment of it; I've had a rough time, yet they haven't finished me off; many things have made me sad, yet I've been a very happy man.

From Paul's letter to the Galatians

(based on Galatians 5:16, 17, 20, 22-23)

Let the Holy Spirit guide all that you say and do.

What our selfish selves want is the opposite of what the Holy Spirit wants.

Selfishness keeps us from being the kind of people the Spirit wants us to be.

When we think only of ourselves, we become rivals.

We are jealous of one another and bad-tempered.

We fight and disagree and get angry.

We become enemies and divide up into groups

and form gangs who hate one another.

People who behave like this do not know what the Kingdom of God is about.

But if the Holy Spirit guides us, we live in love, joy and peace.

We are patient, kind, full of goodness, trust, gentleness, faithfulness and self-control.

Spreading the Good News

FROM PAUL'S LETTER TO THE EPHESIANS

(based on Ephesians 1:20-23)

Let me remind you how we know the power of God:

God raised Jesus to new life.

We can say his place is 'at God's right hand'.

He is the one who is to take charge
of all things and all people.

God has made him Head of the Church,
and the Church is full of his life and his love.

And his name 'Jesus' is to be the best known,
loved and honoured of all names
not just for now but forever.

> *God raised Jesus to new life:*
>
> *For the disciples and the first Christians, this was proof that Jesus was the Messiah sent by God his Father.*

AN EARLY CHRISTIAN HYMN (based on Ephesians 1:3-6)

Give thanks to God, the Father of Jesus.

Give thanks to the Father who has given us the Son.

Give thanks to God who has blessed us
with all the blessings of heaven through Jesus.

Before the world was made, God planned this best of gifts.

From the very beginning God's plan for us was this:
by giving us Jesus to make us sons and daughters, too.

We are God's children, blessed and loved like Jesus the Son.

All the wonder of God's love and life is ours through Jesus.

Give thanks to God the Father who has given us the Son.

Spreading the Good News

From Paul's Letter to the Philippians

(based on Philippians 1:12-17,19)

My friends, I am in prison now, waiting for my trial. But this is not stopping the spreading of the Good News of Jesus. Rather it is making the Good News more widely known. Everybody here knows that I am in prison and why. Even the soldiers who guard the praetorium, where the governor lives, know that I am a friend of Jesus. The other friends here are stronger because I am in prison, and are spreading the news without fear. I am happy and will continue to be happy because I have your prayers and the Spirit of Jesus to strengthen me.

God is very near

(based on Philippians 4:4-9)

Be happy! I'm going to say it again.

Be joyful – always!

God is very near.

Don't worry about anything.

Instead, ask God for what you need.

Pray with a grateful heart knowing how much God loves you;
and the peace of God, which is greater than we can understand,
will fill your minds and hearts and keep you safe and close to Jesus.

Finally, my sisters and brothers,
fill your minds with everything that is true, right, just, good and beautiful,
everything that we love, admire and praise.

Go on doing all that you learned from me and all I have said and done.
And the God who gives us peace will be with you always.

Spreading the Good News

From Paul's Letter to the Colossians

(based on Colossians 3:10-11)

You are created by God to be like God.

You are God's people, his saints. He loves you.

You are all different.

You come from different places,
speak in different ways, have different customs.

But the important thing is that you are God's children.

So love one another, help one another,
be at peace with one another.
And let the love of Jesus fill your hearts and minds.

You are a Holy People

(based on Colossians 3:12-17)

God loves you and has chosen you.

You are a holy people.

You must be full of thoughtfulness for others, generous, gentle and patient.

Put up with one another; be ready to forgive each other if something goes wrong.
The Lord has forgiven you.
You must do the same.
And, most important of all, love each other.
And may the peace of Christ fill your hearts.
This is why you belong to the Christian family.

Always be thankful.
Remember the wonderful words of Jesus.
Be ready to teach and help each other, sharing what you know.
Be happy and enjoy singing hymns to God.
And in everything you say or do, do it as Jesus would want you to,
giving thanks to God the Father.

Spreading the Good News

From Paul's Letter to the Thessalonians

(based on 1 Thessalonians 5:12-18)

Dear Friends,
Help everyone who works hard for you.
Love and respect them for what they do.
Get on well with one another.
Encourage others to work hard.
Help people who are afraid.
Take care of those who are not very strong.
Be patient with everyone.
Make sure you and your friends don't try
to get your own back.

Always do what is best for you, and for everyone else.
Most of all, be happy. Pray, every day.
Make sure you say thank you to God
for all the good things God gives to you.
This is what God wants for you.

From Paul's Letter to Titus

(based on Titus 3:4-7)

God is kindness itself.

God loves us all.
We don't have to do anything to make God love us.

God just loves us all the time.
When we were baptised, God gave us the spirit of love.
We became friends of Jesus and members of his family.

One day we will be happy with God forever.

Spreading the Good News

From the First Letter of Peter

(based on 1 Peter 1:1, 3, 8)

Grace and peace be with you.

Blessed be God the Father
of our Lord Jesus Christ
who has made us his children
by raising Jesus from the dead.

You did not see Jesus, but you love him,
and even without seeing him
you are filled with joy because you believe.

From the First Letter of John

(based on 1 John 3:1-3)

Just think about what great love

God the Father has for us –
God calls us his children.

And that is what we are!

My dear friends,
we are already God's children.
And we know that when we see God,
we will be like God.

We will see God as God really is.

Because we know this,
we try to be loving and kind, as God is.

Because we are close to God,
we keep away from all that is wrong.

Spreading the Good News

THE BOOK OF REVELATION

The Book of Revelation is the last book in the Bible. It was written towards the end of the first century AD, probably by John, the beloved disciple of Jesus, and perhaps added to by some of John's own disciples.

When we know why the Book of Revelation was written and what was happening to the Church in those days, we understand it better.

Towards the end of the first century, the persecution was terrible indeed, all over the Roman Empire. Not everyone was brave enough to suffer the dreadful torture and die in agony for the sake of belief in Jesus. Some fell away and offered incense before pagan gods.

John was exiled to the island of Patmos. He wrote his book of Revelation to show how, in spite of everything, Jesus would keep his promise never to abandon those who believed in him, even when evil seemed to win.

Towards the very end, there is one 'picture' full of hope for those who were suffering persecution.

It describes the New Jerusalem, the heavenly city. In a vision, John sees the end of the world and the beginning of the new world that is to come.

In my mind, I saw this picture…

The Book of Revelation

A New City (based on Revelation 21:1-5)

In my mind, I saw
this picture of a bright new universe.
Nothing bad is in it.

I saw a beautiful new city.
Everything was prepared
ready for people to live in it.

And I heard a great voice which said:
God has come to live with you here.
God will make a home among you.
You will be God's people,
and God will be your God.

God will take away all your sadness
and wipe the tears from your eyes.
There will be no more hurt,
no more pain,
no more suffering,
no more dying;
For all these things are finished and gone.

And the great voice said,
"Write all this down – you can trust what I say."

> What have you learned from these letters about the first Christians?
>
> How is their life the same as the life of Christians today?
>
> What is different?

The Book of Revelation

Welcome

Dear Friends,

One of the priceless treasures that we possess as Christians is that we know our story. We know where we have come from, and to where we are called to go. We know that we share in the story of those who have gone before us, for we play our part in 'God's Story'.

I am sure that *God's Story* will help children and their families to appreciate the riches of the story of God's love that the Scriptures unfold. The story of those people who lived close to God before Jesus came helps us to understand his story better, and his story throws light on what came before him. God's Story is the story of God's love for us in Jesus Christ, the Son of God, a story which encompasses our story now.

One good test of a book written for children is whether it helps tired adult eyes to see things more clearly. I know that *God's Story* will help bring both children and grown-ups into a living relationship with Jesus Christ if it is read with faith and love.

† Edwin Regan
Bishop Emeritus
Former Chairman of the National Project

Notes for Adults

INTRODUCTION

God comes to us, and we come to the mystery of God through one another. The Scriptures are the Word of God. The deep mysteries of God are entrusted to people and handed on from generation to generation. God's Story presents God to children through the eyes and words of the People who believe in God: the People of the first covenant and the People of the new covenant.

The 'Notes for Adults' will help those who share these books with younger children to encourage their understanding and learning. Kati Teague's illustrations provide a rich setting for the text and food for the eye and the imagination. Children will learn that the Bible is a library of books written by many hands: the story-tellers of Genesis, psalmists, prophets and wise scholars. They will come to understand that faith overflows in songs of joy and struggles in times of darkness, clinging to hope. They will learn about the different ways each of the gospels presents Jesus and hear the words of Jesus treasured, remembered and handed on through the early Church.

THE BOOK OF GENESIS (pp.7-17)

(Please also use p.161 – 'Using the photos and illustrations')

Background

The first book of the Bible is Genesis. 'Genesis' is a Greek word meaning 'becoming' or 'beginning to be made'. Genesis is the first of the five books of the 'torah'. Torah means 'teaching', and in the Hebrew Bible, these five books are also called the five books of Moses. In Greek, these five books are called the Pentateuch, 'the five-volume book'.

Different strands of stories are woven together in the book of Genesis.

They tell us about a world and a special way of life, which God offered to chosen people.

They tell of the Holy God the people worship.

They speak of the mystery of God who is greater than anyone can know.

REVERENCE FOR GOD'S WORD

The Church hears and reveres the Bible as God's Word. Children learn reverence for the book of the Bible by seeing adults handle it with care and respect.

Help children to make connections between what they read in *God's Story* and the Bible.

- Place a Bible (not a children's version) in a special place, for example on a table, or cushion or stand. Explain that this is the special book about God that they will read themselves when they are older. Perhaps light a candle as a sign of God's presence and love. Explain that God's Story is to help children to hear good news about God.
- Children can be shown the Lectionary and the Book of the Gospels used in church and a Sunday missal.
- Children can be introduced to the responses used in the Liturgy of the Word at Mass. The reader proclaims 'The Word of the Lord' and the people respond 'Thanks be to God'.

At the end of the Gospel, the priest or deacon proclaims 'The Gospel of the Lord' and the people respond 'Praise to you, Lord Jesus Christ'.

They remind people that each person is made in the image of God.

Religious Education in Primary Schools focuses on God the Creator and Loving Father of the People (Old Testament), and of Jesus Christ (New Testament). In Secondary Schools, pupils study the story of the origin of sin found in Genesis Chapter 3 and the doctrine of original sin as developed in the Latin Church, principally by St Augustine of Hippo (354-430 AD).

Creation (Genesis 1-2)

The Book of Genesis is not meant to be a scientific account of how the world began. Chapter One of Genesis is a beautiful poem about **creation**, which tells us about the goodness and power of God. People of every time, in every place, have been struck by the beauty of the world and wondered about its beginnings.

Today, science and technology enable us to see and know the world in such detail, that the authors of Genesis did not have.

Chapter Two of Genesis tells of humans being made to be like God and to be stewards of God's world. Marriage and the Sabbath day are gifts of God.

Talk and Think
Some questions to explore with children:

- What does this poem tell you about the writer?
- What questions do you think he asked about the world?
- What did he believe about the world?
- What did he want people to know about God?
- What are some ways people can look at the world today that the author of Genesis could not? (from space, etc.)
- How do all the different gifts of creation help us and make us happy?
- How can we care for God's world?
- How might you make Sunday a day to give thanks for all God's gifts?

The Church celebrates
The creation story is read each year at the Easter Vigil when the Church celebrates the new creation in Jesus, followed by the story of Abraham, our father in faith.

Abraham and his Family (pp.12-17: Genesis 12-47)

Background
Genesis tells of God's covenant with Abraham. This **covenant** is the foundation for the faith of the People of the Old and New Testaments. The stories of Abraham and his family tell of a close relationship with God and an unshakeable belief in God's faithfulness. The long lifetimes of these early fathers and mothers of the people are a symbol of God's blessing.

Talk and Think
For each story (Abraham and Sarah, Isaac and Rebecca, Jacob and Joseph) encourage children to think and talk about:

- What did God ask of the person(s)?
- How did the person(s) respond?
  - What does the story tell you about God?
  - What does it tell you about the person's relationship with God?
  - What does it tell you about the writer?
  - What special part does each person play in the story of God's people?

Words to notice
Creation: all that is made by God and depends on God.

Created: specially made by God out of love.

Creator: a name for God, which reminds us that everything and everyone is made by God.

Covenant: a solemn agreement which strengthens a relationship. God promised that Abraham would be the father of a great nation. Abraham promised to serve the One God. Another word for 'covenant' is 'testament'. The Old and New Testaments form the Christian Bible. Jewish people speak of the Hebrew Scriptures while Christians speak of the Old Testament.

THE BOOKS OF EXODUS, DEUTERONOMY AND LEVITICUS
(pp.18-31)

Background
'Exodus' means 'going out'.

The story of how God saved them and led them to freedom is very important for the Chosen People. In telling the story, in remembering and celebrating God's love, the People proclaim their faith in God's love and faithfulness. Moses is the one chosen by God to lead the people.

Deuteronomy is written as if it were a collection of speeches or sermons given by Moses.

He reminds the people that God loves them and has blessed them. They are to remember this and love and obey God so that they may have life and continue to be blessed by their God. The key words in this book are: "Love the Lord your God with all your heart, with all your soul and with all your strength."

Leviticus is the book of priestly rules of the tribe of Levi. It is written as if these laws were given to Moses.

Moses
Moses was born in Egypt at a time when God's People were slaves, and all boy babies born to Israelite families were taken away at birth. Moses' mother hid him in a basket among the reeds on the riverbank. The Pharaoh's daughter found him there and brought him up herself. When he grew up, he found out that he was an Israelite, and his people were slaves. Soon after that he left

Egypt and joined a family of nomads in the desert. These wandering people had flocks of sheep and goats, and so Moses became a shepherd.

God knew how hard life was for the Israelites. God chose Moses to go back to Egypt and tell Pharaoh to set his people free. The special meal they ate on the night of their escape became a celebration of what God did to save them from slavery in Egypt.

Moses and the Israelites camped near Mount Sinai. The giving of the Law – God's rules, the commandments – at Sinai is a renewal of the covenant. God renewed the promise to Abraham, and the people committed themselves to a new way of life as God's People.

Talk and Think
Exodus
Help children to focus on:

- **The people and their needs**
- **God's actions and blessings – the law, food on the journey, a land of their own**
- **How the story is remembered, told and celebrated and handed on.**

Leviticus and Deuteronomy
Help children to focus on:

- **The people's respect for the law as God's gift to them**
- **How the law helps them to live as God's people**
- **What does the law have to say that helps people today to live in God's way.**

The Church celebrates
At the Easter Vigil, Christians listen to the story of the Passover in preparation for the Mass of Easter Night and the celebration of Jesus' Passover – God his Father frees him from death and gives him new life. He frees us from the slavery of sin and calls us to new life.
(First Reading of the Mass of Easter Night, Romans 6:6-7)

Note: *For Jewish believers, Passover is the great celebration of the Exodus.*

THE BOOKS OF SAMUEL AND THE KINGS (pp.32-39)

Background
The Books of Samuel and the Judges are among six historical books – Joshua, Judges, 1 and 2 Samuel and 1 and 2 Kings.

They tell of God's People and their leaders and of the challenges and joys of living in God's way. *God's Story 3* focuses on Samuel, David and Solomon.

The Book of Ruth tells the story of Ruth and David. She was the foreigner who chose to follow God's way and became the ancestor of David, one of the best-loved of the kings who led God's People.

Talk and Think
Help children to focus on:

- **God's call and how this comes to the person(s)**
- **the response of the person(s)**
- **what has been remembered and handed on about the person(s)**
- **what does the story say about God and about living in God's way?**

THE BOOK OF PSALMS (pp.40-52)

Background
The Book of Psalms contains 150 prayer songs.

Mary and Joseph were faithful Jews, and Jesus grew up learning and living the Jewish tradition. He would have known the Psalms well and prayed them regularly.

The Jewish people and the Church have used the Psalms through many centuries.

The Psalms have been grouped as:

Pilgrimage Psalms – 84, 118, 122

Prayers for help – 6, 22, 44, 130

Psalms of trust in God's love – 23, 46, 136, 146

Creation Psalms – 49, 65, 98, 104, 139

Praise and Thanksgiving – 100

David
Some Psalms are described 'Of David', and it may be that he was their author. David is remembered as Israel's greatest king. He was a singer and played the harp. The Bible tells us that with his music he was able to soothe King Saul when the king

was depressed. You might like to encourage children to imagine how David might have come to write *Ps 139*.

Talk and Think

Help children to notice the different ways the psalmists describe God and God's love.

Encourage children to find images and reminders of God at home, at school and in the world around them.

Encourage children to use words of the psalms as morning and night prayers.

The Church celebrates

Today a psalm is prayed in the **Liturgy of the Word** at Mass.

All priests, many religious and many lay people pray psalms at regular times each day as part of the **Prayer of the Church**.

Words to notice

Liturgy of the Word: At Mass, we listen to the Word of the Lord. We say 'Thanks be to God'. The readings come from the Old and New Testaments. We stand to greet the Gospel. We hear the Word of God. We say 'Praise to you, Lord Jesus Christ'.

Prayer of the Church: Psalms, readings and prayers prayed at special times each day by the Church all over the world.

THE WISDOM BOOKS (pp.53-57)

Background

Six books of the Bible are grouped under this heading: Proverbs, Ecclesiastes, Song of Songs, Wisdom, Ecclesiasticus and Job.

The Book of Ecclesiasticus is also called the Book of Ben Sira. He was a devout Jewish scholar. He wants his reader to remember that God will teach anyone how to be wise who asks sincerely.

Talk and Think

Help children to focus on:

- **What does the writer say about God?**
- **What does the passage tell us about ourselves as human beings?**
- **What does it tell us about living in God's way?**
- **What do you like in this reading and why?**

BOOKS OF THE PROPHETS (pp.58-67)

Background

A prophet is one who hears the word of God and passes it on with courage and conviction. Each prophet shares something special about God. There are 17 books in the Bible that bear the names of prophets. This does not mean they were the authors of the books. Often their words were written down by others because they were so greatly treasured.

God's Story 3 focuses on seven prophets:

Isaiah – in the book of Isaiah the writings of three different prophets are found under this one name. But all share concern about the holiness of God, the faithfulness of God and the hope this gives.

Jeremiah and Ezekiel were the prophets of the exile. They encouraged the people at this difficult time in their history.

Hosea and Joel portray the faithfulness of God and God's inexhaustible love.

Amos challenges God's People to be true to God's ways.

Zephaniah's challenge includes encouragement to look forward to the great things God will do.

Talk and Think

Help children to focus on:

- **What does the prophet tell us about God?**
- **How is this good news for the people?**
- **What does the prophet want the people to do?**
- **What do you like in this reading and why?**

THE NEW TESTAMENT – THE GOSPELS

Background

The four Gospels are the most important books of the New Testament. 'Gospel' comes from the Anglo-Saxon word for 'good news'. The gospel writers are called evangelists, from a Greek word which means tellers of good news. Each evangelist wants his readers to hear the good news and believe in Jesus.

But, before ever it was written, the gospel of Jesus was spread by word of mouth. Each evangelist wrote for a particular Christian community and drew on the richness of the oral tradition in doing so.

Many scholars now agree that Mark's was the earliest gospel to be written. Matthew and Luke seem to have used Mark's gospel and added to it. John's gospel was probably the last to be written.

The Gospels in God's Story 3
The Coming of Jesus (pp.69-81)
This section begins with Luke and Matthew's stories, then the beginning of the gospels of Mark and John.

Talk and Think
Help children to notice what the texts say about Jesus and what he will be and do for God's People.

Look back to the passages from the prophet Isaiah (pp. 59-65).

What clues can they find to show why the Church interprets these as descriptions of Jesus?

Zechariah, Elizabeth and John, Mary and Joseph were chosen to prepare for the coming of Jesus. Help children to notice the different ways in which Luke shows how each one recognises God's call and respond.

The Church celebrates
During Advent, the Church remembers how God prepared for the coming of Jesus. Help children to revisit the gospel stories of John the Baptist and Mary and Joseph and think about the different ways in which they are part of God's plan. How, during Advent, might the children prepare for the coming of Jesus? Help them to remember that Advent celebrates the coming of Jesus at Bethlehem, today and at the end of time.

The account of the flight into Egypt is the prescribed Gospel reading for the Feast of the Holy Family (Cycle A). This feast is celebrated on the Sunday within the octave of Christmas. The Presentation and Finding in the Temple are the prescribed Gospel readings for Cycles B and C.

The Church prays
The first part of the Hail Mary is based on Luke's accounts of what God's angel messenger and Elizabeth said to Mary.

Pray the Hail Mary with the children.

Use Mary's praise and Zechariah's as morning and evening prayers.

The Joyful Mysteries of the Rosary are based on Chapters 1-2 of Luke's Gospel.

The Gospel according to Matthew (pp.82-88)
The focus is on Jesus, the Teacher. Chapters 5-7 in Matthew's gospel form what is called the Sermon on the Mount. For Matthew's Jewish readers this would bring reminders of Mount Sinai and the giving of the Law. Jesus invites his followers to go further in faithfulness to the law.

Talk and Think
Help children to notice how Jesus invites people to 'go further'.

Some questions to explore:

- **How would the people who heard Jesus have felt?**
- **Can you think of some who would be especially happy? Nervous? Afraid?**
- **What is your favourite text/line?**
- **How does it make you feel?**
- **Is there anyone you think would be happy to hear Jesus' words today? Why?**
- **Is there anything in the world you think would change if people remembered Jesus' words? Why?**

The Gospel according to Mark (pp.89-93)
The focus is on how Jesus came to proclaim the kingdom of God and what it means to be a follower of Jesus and a kingdom person. The disciples' expectations of the kingdom arose from their experience of being subjects in the great Roman Empire. They hoped Jesus would change their world by taking power for himself and that they would share in it.

Help children to notice how Jesus invites people to follow him and the different responses. What does Jesus say about being a 'kingdom person'? (a friend/follower of Jesus, keeps the commandments, puts others first, serves others)

Help children to think of what kind of world they want for themselves.

Talk and Think
Some questions to explore:

- **What does Jesus say about being a kingdom person?**
- **What did his friends find hard to understand?**
- **Why do you think this was hard for them?**
- **What do you think you would have to do to be a kingdom person?**
- **What would you find easy?**

- **What would you find hard?**

The Gospel according to Luke (pp.94-104)

The focus is on God's call and God's plan. Luke shows how Jesus chooses God's way and begins his mission. The passages selected from Luke's gospel show the coming of Jesus is good news for individual people. They find new life through Jesus. In Luke's story of the beginning, good news comes to and through particular men and women: Zachariah, Mary, Elizabeth, Anna and Simeon. Many of Luke's people are 'people on the margins'. For example, Levi and Zacchaeus were tax-collectors. The shepherds, who are the first to hear the good news, represent the poor and the marginalised.

The parables of the Good Samaritan (p.100) and the Prodigal Son (p.102) are found only in Luke's gospel. For Jewish listeners, the Samaritans were heretics who did not worship God in the true way.

Help children to think of the kind of person who would be a 'shocking good neighbour' today. The parable of the 'prodigal' father and son provides an opportunity to talk about family life and forgiveness.

Talk and Think

For each text talk about what Jesus did, what he said, how people responded.

Some questions to explore:

- **How did the person(s) feel about meeting Jesus?**
- **What did they do?**
- **How was Jesus 'good news' for the person?**
- **How did the life of the person change?**
- **How do other people react? (the Pharisees and scribes, the disciples, the older brother)**
- **What does the story tell us about Jesus? About God his Father?**
- **How does the message make you feel?**
- **What would you have done?**
- **How could Jesus' message help change your life now?**

The Church celebrates and prays

The 'Our Father' (p.104) is the prayer of all disciples of Jesus, the family prayer of the Church. It is the opening prayer of the Rite of Communion at Mass. How might this be reflected in the way the 'Our Father' is prayed at home and in school?

The Gospel according to John (pp.105-111)

The focus is on Jesus, the Word of God. Jesus makes God known by everything he does and says. His invitation is **'Come and see'**. He is new life for the world. The imagery of bread and the vine emphasise this. Chapters 14-17 are a wonderful summary of the theme of Love in John's gospel. Jesus' words and prayers express his love for his Father and his disciples and his heart's desire that they should know and share this love.

Talk and Think

Help children to notice how Jesus' words and actions are about living a full and free life.

Some questions to explore:

- **What do the images of bread and the vine say about Jesus?**
- **What do they say about being a friend of Jesus?**
- **What does Jesus say and do that shows he wants his friends to live a full and free life?**

THE GREATEST WEEK (pp.112-124)

Background

Passion Sunday, also called Palm Sunday marks the beginning of Holy Week. The Church calls this the 'greatest week', the celebration of the greatest 'mystery': the death and resurrection of Jesus. The Church enters into the mystery of God's love, and faithfulness revealed in Jesus **crucified**, a love greater than the human mind can grasp. It calls Christians to celebrate God who enters into the pain and fear of death and transforms human sorrow to joy and death into new life. The focus is on the story as told in Mark's gospel and the different details added in the other gospels.

Talk and Think

Help children to follow the events through the week and to notice how the story unfolds through the four gospels.

Some questions to explore for each event:

- **What does Jesus say and do?**
- **Who else plays a part in the event? How?**
- **What does this say about Jesus?**
- **What does it say about being a friend of Jesus?**
- **What do you think you would have done?**

- How would you have felt feel?
- What words will you remember?

The Church celebrates

The events of Palm Sunday are celebrated on Passion Sunday. For the first time in Holy Week, the whole account of the passion of Jesus is read, in Year A from Matthew, Year B from Mark and Year C from Luke. On Good Friday the whole account of the passion is read from John.

At the Mass of the Lord's Supper on Holy Thursday John's account of the washing of the feet is the gospel reading.

Holy Saturday is the only day in the year when there is no Eucharist. The tabernacle and font are empty. The Church keeps vigil until the Easter gospel is proclaimed. The revival of adult baptisms is a powerful symbol of the new life that comes to the world in the risen Christ.

Words to notice

Crucified: The Romans put slaves and criminals to death by nailing or tying them to a cross. A crucifix is a cross with a figure of Jesus on it. Christians remember the love of Jesus who died on the cross out of love for God his Father and all the peoples of the world.

THE EMPTY TOMB (pp.125-127) and NEW LIFE (pp.128-130)

Background

No one saw the moment of the resurrection. All four Gospel accounts refer to the empty tomb, but the differences reflect something of the first shock and confusion. The disciples receive the news with a mixture of fear, bewilderment, faith and joy. Luke's story of the disciples on the road to Emmaus shows how, for the disciples as for all Christians the journey to faith is a gradual discovery of Jesus present in daily life, in Scripture, and in the Breaking of Bread. The forty days of resurrection time are symbolic like the forty years of the Exodus journey. The Church grows in understanding of the risen Jesus and its mission.

Talk and Think

Help children to notice how the friends of Jesus grew in faith.

Some questions to explore:

- How did the friends of Jesus feel?
- What did they do?
- What happened when they met Jesus?
- What was Jesus' message to them?

THE ACTS OF THE APOSTLES
(pp.131-139)

Background

The foundation for Luke's second book is unshakeable conviction that Jesus died, that God his Father raised him to new life and that the apostles are witnesses to him. After the Ascension, the disciples were fearful. They held on to Jesus' promise that he would send the Holy Spirit to be their teacher and guide. Pentecost, the coming of the Holy Spirit, is the event which confirms their faith. The symbolic language of wind and fire emphasises the transforming power of this experience. The disciples are 'on fire' to spread the good news. Pentecost comes from a Greek word meaning the 'fiftieth' day. At this feast, the Jewish people celebrated God's gift of the law. Luke's account makes it clear that the Good News of Jesus is for the whole world. He tells of peoples from all over the world who had come to celebrate the festival and who heard the word of God in their own languages. The power of the Holy Spirit is for all Christians, and all are called to share the mission to spread the gospel message.

Note: The picture language of the New Testament accounts of the Ascension express the belief of the early Christian-Jewish community that God's dwelling place was above the heavens. It is important to respect the metaphorical language of the text and not leave children with the impression that heaven is a place 'up there'. 'Heaven is a state and not a place.'
(Blessed John Paul II, November 1999)

Talk and Think

Help children to notice how the power of the Holy Spirit is seen in changed lives.

Some questions to explore:

- **What changes can you find? (in people's feelings, words, actions)**
- How did others react? (the crowds at Pentecost, the people in Jerusalem, their leaders) How did the friends of Jesus spread the good news? (words, actions)

- How did people respond?
  (the Ethiopian, Lydia)

SPREADING THE GOOD NEWS
(pp.140-149)

Background
Paul is a key figure in the early Church. The majority of the New Testament letters are from Paul to the Churches he had founded or visited. **Corinth** was a great cosmopolitan city in Greece. In his letters to the Corinthians Paul is stern in dealing with problems and encouraging too. The church in **Colossae** was not one of those founded by Paul, but when he heard news of the Christians there, he wrote to encourage and advise them. In the letter to the **Romans** Paul says how much he looks forward to going to Rome and meeting the Christians there. **Galatia** was an area in what is now known as Turkey. **Thessalonica** was a port north of Athens. The two letters to the Thessalonians, which are contained in the New Testament, are probably the earliest letters of Paul, written less than 30 years after the death and resurrection of Jesus. The letters from Peter and John show the good news is the same throughout the early Church.

Talk and Think
Help children to image the people who received the letters.

Imagine you are one of the people who received Paul's letter.

- **What part of the letter do you like best? Why?**
- **What will you remember most of all? Why?**

THE BOOK OF REVELATION (pp.150-151)

Background
This is the last book of the Bible. It looks forward to the time when God's plans will be complete, and God's People will live with God forever. It is an example of apocalyptic writing. This uses signs and symbols to express faith in God's love and power. It was probably written to encourage Christians in a time of persecution.

The focus is on the vision of God's 'new city'.

Talk and Think
Help children to express their own hopes and dreams.

Some questions to explore:

- **How do you think people reading this would feel?**
- **How do you feel?**
- **What words about God do you like best? Why?**
- **What words will you try to remember? Why?**

Using the photos and illustrations

The photographs and illustrations have been carefully selected and designed to support children's learning. Please use them when sharing the text with children. They can be:

- a starting point
- a prompt for 'second thoughts'
- a way to develop ideas
- a reminder.

For example:

p.13   The pictures of the Bedouin might be a starting point for talking about the nomadic life. For a desert nomad like Abraham, the sand and stars are powerful symbols of how richly God's promise would be fulfilled. Similarly, the pictures on p25 will help to deepen understanding of the desert life.

p.21   The picture of refugees today helps to relate to the Exodus and the search for a homeland and also be a talking point about the many who are exiles from their homelands today.

pp.44-45   These pictures can help to make connections between the psalms and experiences of life today.

pp.50-51   These pictures might help children to find images in their own lives to illustrate.

& 56-57   Lines from the Psalms. A use for family photo albums/videos perhaps.

New Testament illustrations

Each illustration focuses closely on the person or persons at a key moment. Encourage children to think about how the art has imagined and pictured the feelings and response of each person.

For example:

pp.78-79   Simeon's joy, Mary and Joseph's bewilderment, the attentiveness of the scholars to the boy Jesus.

p.97   The reactions of the disciples, the calm expectation/authority in Jesus' gesture.

p.103   What the drooping shoulders and outstretched arms of the figures express.

p.124   The different figures at the foot of the cross.

p.126-7   The before and after emotions of the women; notice also the changing sky.